Dances with Veils

'A Journey to the Divine Feminine'

By Mezdulene Bliss

Dance is an expression of
what my soul is feeling.

When I dance, my body and
spirit are joined in a
personal expression of the
essence of who I am.

Dance allows me to express
and release emotions which
otherwise must be curbed in
everyday life.

I can experience the joy it is
to be a woman.

-author unknown

For my daughter, Avena.

Her presence in my life has given me the strength

to endure.

Her belief in me has given me the inspiration to succeed.

I cherish her existence, celebrate her essence

and love her from the depths of my soul.

CONTENTS

FOREWORD

Once upon a time when I stepped into my first belly dance class, shy, inhibited, self-conscious and lacking in self-esteem and awareness, or in other words, just plain fearful, I had no way of knowing the enormity of the step I was taking. I had no way of knowing that I would be consumed by a passion that would span the next several decades, no way of knowing that this beautiful art form was to become my ticket to healing and wholeness.

My journey with belly dance has been filled with all aspects of emotion, but the prevailing emotion has been joy and at times bliss and even rapture.

You might wonder how this can be, how a mere dance can be so life-altering, and this is the story I am going to tell you. It's my story, but also the story of the dance, the story of the most amazing community of women, my students and friends and most of all the story of healing.

So far, my dance journey has spanned over three decades, years of personal growth as well as adventures. The dance has been my anchor through my deepest pain. It has also been joyful fun and everything in between.

Sharing the dance through performing has been a spiritual experience as well as an ecstatic one. Sharing the dance through teaching has been enriching and profound. Watching my students come to the dance as I did, fearful and beaten down by the world and then blossoming into confident and beautiful performers has been the most rewarding experience I can imagine.

My work is with women. Over time I began to understand the power in our femininity, and I began to connect more and more to my own Divine Femininity. Our dance is sacred. As we dance, we do the same movements that women have done for thousands of years. We do the same movements as women are doing all over the planet and the same movements that women will continue to do for thousands of years.

The Native Americans talk about how what we do today will impact the seventh generation which was a concept that made sense to me, but one I didn't really understand until I realized that through the dance, what I'm doing now will have an impact seven generations from now.

As a teacher of the dance, I will live on through my students as they become teachers and their students become teachers and onward. In fact, I already know dancers who are students of my student's students.

My dance has been a spiritual journey, as well as a physical and emotional one, and as I share my experiences with you I hope that you will be inspired to do whatever it is that makes your soul sing. I hope that you follow your inner guidance and allow yourself to open to the Divine Feminine so that you, too, can become empowered.

1 BEFORE BELLY DANCE

I've always had a knowing inside of myself, something calling me, something speaking to me from another realm. I knew there was something just out of my reach that was intangible, something that if I could just grasp would help me feel complete, would answer my question, "Why am I here?"

Even as a small child, I felt this calling, a Spiritual awareness that I couldn't quite connect with, didn't understand, just a knowing that there was something beyond what I could see and feel, something important.

I realize, now, that this was about connecting to the Divine. I had an innate sense of spirituality but no words or experience in this lifetime to know what this inner longing was about.

This is my story; one that I hope inspires others to live their dreams. There is nothing special about me, and if I can do it, anyone can. This is a story about what belly dance has given me, and while some may find it an unusual tool for healing, it is profound, not just for me, but also for many thousands of women around the world, women from all backgrounds, all walks of life, all countries, cultures and traditions with one common bond, belly dance.

I used to live in a world of fear. I was controlled by it, and crippled by it. When the phone rang, my heart would start to race as anxiety set in. I couldn't even order a taco at Taco Bell. I used to be afraid to drive, afraid to meet strangers; you name it, and I was afraid of it.

This wasn't a good way to live. I hated it, hated myself, and hated my life. I hated being shy and fearful, but I didn't have a clue how to change things, how to find peace.

My childhood was filled with abuse and neglect. I was molested by my uncle and then beaten half to death by my father because it was 'my fault.' I was four years old. It wasn't until I had my own child that I understood how sick and damaged my parents were. When my daughter was four, I remembered what had happened to me and wondered how anyone could hurt such a small and innocent being. She was so precious to me, and I would have given my life to protect her from harm, and the thought of harming her myself was beyond comprehension. Every day of her childhood I told her how much I loved her.

As a young child I was repeatedly sexually and physically abused, but it was the neglect and the words that caused me the most harm. So many times my parents said they wished they'd never had me, wished that I had died at birth, that I was filthy, a horrible daughter, they were ashamed and embarrassed of me, etc. They showered my little sisters with attention and love but I was either ignored or abused by both my father and my mother. I constantly tried to gain their approval. In fifth grade I worked hard and was so excited to bring home a report card with straight A's. I joyfully ran to my dad and showed him. His response was simply, "Why aren't they A pluses?" My heart fell, and I was completely devastated. It was at that moment I knew there was nothing I could do to gain his approval and I gave up. With no words of love or approval as a child, it's no wonder I crawled into my own personal shell and was afraid to come out. No wonder depression became a life-time companion.

As a teenager I was filled with even more pain and angst. I longed to escape what felt like torture living in a home without love where I was constantly under some form of attack.

I fell in love with my first husband, when I was sixteen and left home at seventeen to go to the same college he attended. For the first time, I felt loved, felt important to someone, and we got married on my eighteenth birthday. There was no long white gown or fancy reception and celebration, just the two of us at the courthouse with the justice of peace and a couple of witnesses. It was quick and simple, but we were in love and we didn't need or want a fancy ceremony. We just wanted to be together.

At the end of my first college term we decided to drop out, eager to create a life together. We chose to move to Oregon where we bought a parcel of land surrounded by hundreds of acres owned by the Bureau of Land Management commonly known as BLM. We had 11 acres on the side of a small mountain, straight up and down. We hired a guy with a bull dozer to come in and scrape away and create a flat space of dirt. Then, with the bulldozer, he pulled our 35 foot trailer (purchased with my life savings) onto that spot of dirt. We were nestled in among huge, old, large leaf maples, with the mountain above us and a tiny valley of wild delphiniums below us. I could never have imagined a place so beautiful. Our trailer was surrounded by dirt which quickly turned into mud as the rains started.

That first winter was very hard. We had only been to Oregon in the summer when it was sunny, warm and green, not hot and barren like the desert we were from. We didn't know about the rain.

Our spot carved out of the hillside was up a long and steep driveway. We had to 'buy' rock to put on the driveway, another new experience for us. In Arizona you could drive all over the desert without any problem. I'd never heard of buying gravel for a road, because everything was gravel and rough sand where we came from.

One day, we came home from grocery shopping, and our driveway was flooded. Water was pouring down the tire ruts of the steep climb like two waterfalls. The creek at the bottom of our property was overflowing the culvert. The waterfalls were coming down the hill and pouring into the creek which was now running deeply across the bottom of the driveway. So, we grabbed our grocery bags and waded hip-deep across the flooding waters and hiked up our driveway between the waterfalls to our home.

It turns out it was an unusually wet winter, but we didn't know that, and we wondered what the heck we were doing here in the middle of the woods slogging through a flood to our home. And, we wondered if the rain was ever going to stop.

But, this lifestyle suited me. I was very isolated, so I didn't have to deal with people. My husband worked and was gone long hours leaving me home alone. I remember being lonely occasionally, but mostly I kept busy. I made beautiful gardens, and I enjoyed creating many things such as hanging tables and bean bag chairs to make our home more beautiful and comfortable. I also spent many long hours making quilts and creating artwork, something I loved doing.

Over time, we gradually built a house around our trailer out of used lumber and old windows from 19th century farm houses. It was our own, uniquely personal, haven in the forest.

For several years, I didn't have to deal with my fears. I rarely went to town, rarely saw people. I didn't know anyone, so the phone didn't ring. My family called only once or twice a year. They were just glad to be rid of me and certainly weren't worried about their oldest daughter moving to the boonies of Oregon.

If I ever doubted my childhood feelings of being unloved by my parents, all doubt ended when I attended my sister's wedding and saw huge stacks of old letters. I thought they were old love letters from her soon-to-be husband, but it turns out they were from my mother. Even though my sister had gone to college only a hundred miles away and was home on weekends, our mother had written to her every single day and called. I had moved over a thousand miles away and had received less only one or two letters or phone calls a year. It was painful, but validated my feelings.

I loved my husband and baby, loved living in the boonies, and made goals of more gardens and more artwork. I had my beautiful daughter and lived what I felt was a perfect lifestyle.

My husband and I decided to start a jewelry-making business together and he talked me into getting a part-time job so that he could stay home and work on starting the business. I ventured out into the world and applied at a tiny mom and pop fabric store. Fabric was something I was comfortable with, and as a teen I had done retail at my parent's trading post, so I had a frame of reference on how to handle this job. I was hired immediately. I liked the job and realized that maybe I had been living too isolated for too long. It felt good to be among people I had something in common with even if it was just sewing.

I worked for just a few short weeks when one day, my world was radically changed, and my life was forever altered.

I remember that it was a Friday, and I was at work. I felt a headache starting, something unusual for me because I rarely got headaches. I took some aspirin and kept working, but the pain grew more and more intense. When it reached the point where it felt like the top of my head was about to explode, I asked to go home early. It was slow that afternoon, so my boss had no problem allowing me to leave.

As I drove home the pain, which I couldn't imagine being any worse, got worse. It reached the point where I had to pull over and get a grip because I was starting to have double vision. After a few minutes, I got myself together, and I finished driving home.

When I pulled into the bottom of our driveway, I saw a car parked at the bottom of the hill. The car belonged to my one female friend, and I immediately knew something was up. There was only one reason the car was parked there. She was afraid to drive up our driveway, so when she came to visit without her husband, she parked at the bottom and walked up the driveway. So, I knew that for some reason she was at my house alone with my husband.

My already exploding head began to pound even harder as I drove up the driveway. It felt like I was being hit with a sledgehammer, blow after blow. My stomach also started to clench like a huge fist squeezing tightly.

I parked my car and walked in the front door, and I knew. So many things hit me at once, the sights and smells and sounds all crashing in on me in a split second. From the entry, I could see my daughter upstairs standing in her crib calling and reaching out for me as I walked in. I smelled incense, saw candles burning, and I heard someone running into the bathroom. I saw my husband quickly pulling on his pants, and seeing the look on his face, I felt my world crumble into a million pieces.

My headache was forgotten. Before I could move, he ran and grabbed me and said something in gibberish about how this didn't matter, how it wasn't love, it was sex, how he loved only me, etc. I felt like I was suffocating, dying and I just wanted to get away. He and I had always been in tune with each other, so he could feel it too, and he hung onto me more and more tightly as if by hanging on he could somehow erase my pain, erase his deed and somehow stop the drama before it got any worse.

Finally, my head cleared for a brief moment, and I felt a fleeting sense of calm. "Could I please have a drink of water?" I asked. It was the only way I could think of to make him let go of me, and it worked. I got a drink of water then ran out of the house before he could react. As I backed my car around the corner to head down the driveway, I heard this frightening keening sound, like a wounded animal screaming. It took a few moments for my brain to realize that the sound was coming from my own throat. It was a surreal moment as a part of me wondered how I could possibly be making such a sound.

As I drove, my only thought was that I wanted to die. I felt worthless and abandoned. I was in shock, and felt as if my life was over. I thought about where I could go to crash and die, but I couldn't come up with anything. I didn't want to hurt anyone else, there were no cliffs close to drive off of and I didn't want to end up just mangled and in physical pain, too. It's really amazing how the mind works when you are in shock, how there is clarity and confusion all at the same time.

I knew I wasn't in any condition to drive very far, and was somehow guided to the house of one of my husband's bachelor friends.

When he came to the door, he took one look at me and poured me a glass of wine. He knew I didn't drink, but he also knew I needed a drink. He asked me what was up, and I told him. He looked at me as if I had told him the Martians had landed and had turned me into an alien life form. He absolutely refused to believe what I was saying. He insisted that I had made a mistake and that there was a perfectly harmless explanation for what I had witnessed. He made me promise to stay at his house while he drove out to talk to my husband, and he poured me another glass of wine.

That night, wine was my friend. I can't stand the taste of the stuff, but that night, I didn't taste a thing. I just needed to be numb.

To finish this part of my story would take a book in itself, but this was the day my life, as I knew it, ended and my unknown new life began. I ended up taking my daughter and leaving my husband for a few months, but then I went back to him believing we could work things through. I still believe we could have, but as it turns out, he didn't believe it, and it takes two to keep a relationship healthy.

Any progress I had made on coming out of my shell was destroyed. I was now, shy plus shell-shocked. What a mess. What a victim I was before I began to belly dance.

Right after I returning to my husband, an acquaintance from down the road came to visit me. She asked me to go to belly dance class with her, and for some reason, I felt compelled to go. Some inner part of me recognized that this was an opportunity that I didn't want to miss.

2 MY BELLY DANCE JOURNEY BEGINS

When I was a child, I dreamed of being a dancer. One day when I was about six years old, my mother took me to a tap dancing demonstration and asked me if I wanted to take a class. I remember asking her, "Will I have to do that?" as I pointed at the dancers on the stage. She told me, "Yes, that's what you will do in class." I remember thinking that I could never do that, not understanding that I would be taught one step at a time. In my mind I thought I would be expected to do what the dancers on stage were doing in my first class. Being extremely shy and fearful, I told my mom I didn't want to take the class, and that was my first and last childhood chance to ever take a dance class.

Because my childhood was so abusive, emotional survival was a priority over any dreams of dancing. My dreams took a more practical turn, the dream of escaping the pain and creating a better life for myself, the dream of someday having children of my own and giving them the love that I yearned to receive and giving them the security and safety that I never had while growing up.

I cherished my first husband with every cell of my being. He was my knight on a white horse and the first person that I ever felt love from. When I was 21, I gave birth to my beautiful daughter, Avena, and it seemed my dream of having my own loving family was a reality. Unfortunately, that reality only lasted for a couple of years.

When my friend, Ishtar, asked me to attend the belly dance class with her, I was not only extremely shy and fearful but also pretty much broken internally. I was like a walking zombie just going through the motions, feeling dead on the inside and smiling on the outside.

I was also very self-conscious, always an overweight child and continuing the weight problem into adulthood.

I hated being so shy, self-conscious and fearful, and in fact, hated myself after having learned from my parents that I had no value and having it re-enforced by my husband's infidelity. That's how I felt at the time, and despondency was my new full-time companion. To put it mildly, I was an emotional wreck and a total mess physically as well.

When Ishtar first approached me, my first inclination was to tell her no. She proceeded to tell me how much fun belly dance was and how she thought I would like it. I have to say that a part of me was intrigued with the idea of belly dancing. I had never seen a belly dancer or knew anything about it, but I was curious and apparently ready to experience something new. Any distraction from my pain was a welcome distraction.

Little did I know that I was about to begin a journey that would span decades and what a gift the dance would be for me and how that gift would change so many lives beyond my own.

I will never forget my very first belly dance class. Ishtar drove over 30 miles up the Oregon coast and then inland along a winding, country road. As we drove, I wondered what the class would be like. I knew nothing about belly dance, so I couldn't even imagine. I began to wonder where we were going, and she finally pulled into the driveway of a nice looking home. We got out of the car, went into the garage and climbed some stairs ending up in a small, but beautiful dance studio. It had a wooden floor, hard and smooth, and one wall was covered with floor to ceiling mirrors. The opposite wall had large windows overlooking the woods. It was as if the huge fir trees were peeking in to see what was going to happen inside this little studio in the middle of their secluded forest.

Ishtar introduced me to our teacher, Kadriyah, a tiny woman with frizzy blonde hair who was wrapped in sparkling fabric. She welcomed me to her class and told me to take a seat. As I looked around, I didn't see any chairs, but the other students were beginning to sit down on the colorful pillows on the studio floor, so I followed suit.

There were about a dozen students, and they were a mixture of women, some younger, some older, some heavy-set, some slim, some short and some tall. They all dressed differently, some in dance leotards, some in pants and some in long skirts. It became clear that this dance was something for women of all ages, sizes and life styles!

Ishtar and the other women were chattering with each other and were obviously looking forward to the class. I was so shy and felt so out of place, and I began to wonder what I'd gotten myself into, so I just sat and watched and listened.

It wasn't long, before Kadriyah turned on some music. Her back was turned as she started the record, yes, a vinyl record back in the day! The music was immediately upbeat and exotic, and I instantly loved it. I'd never heard anything like it before.

After turning the music on, my new teacher turned towards us and began to dance. As she danced, she played a rhythm on a pair of finger cymbals, and they rang quickly and effortlessly. Her hips shimmied as she moved around the room smiling at us, her students, performing for us from her heart and showing us what we had to look forward to learning.

I was completely transfixed as well as transported. I felt entranced by her music and by her movements and felt a deep sense of recognition even though this was the first time I'd ever seen a belly dancer, ever heard such sounds, seen such a costume, or such movements. I felt a welling of emotion and felt like I had come home, like everything in my life had led to this moment. It was almost a sense of déjà vu, but more of an inner knowing that I'd found something I didn't even know I was looking for.

I felt transported in time to a place where I felt at peace and a connection to something that was elusive, yet profound. It was a fleeting feeling at the time, but one that has become stronger and stronger over the years and more solid.

I wanted to belly dance more than anything I had ever wanted to do. I wanted to learn how to do what Kadriyah was doing. I wanted to get my hands on that music so I could listen to it day and night. I wanted to wear a costume and learn everything I possibly could about this new art form.

I couldn't see myself doing it, couldn't even imagine it, but I felt inflamed with a desire I had never before felt. It was the beginning of a consuming passion that I have never been able to tame, a passion that has driven me as well as sustained me through years of life challenges.

During my first few lessons my body felt awkward and uncoordinated, yet at the same time, there were some movements that felt totally natural. It was like learning a new language, a language that was foreign, yet eternal, one that had been spoken since time began and will continue to be spoken into infinity.

Between lessons, Ishtar and I got together and practiced in her living room. She had music, and since she had already taken some classes, she knew the steps. She was a great help for me, and I feel that our practice sessions helped me learn much more quickly than if I had tried remembering the steps and movements by myself. At home I practiced every single day.

Over a period of a few weeks, my body became more and more fit. The first thing I noticed was that my thighs got toned up and firm. I went from flabby thighs to muscular, hard thighs.

When I first started classes I suffered low back pain related to an old injury. I'd had chronic back pain for a couple of years, and at first I was concerned as a lot of the movements involved the low back, pelvis and hips really putting those muscles to test. My back muscles would be so sore after the first few classes, and I questioned whether or not it was a good thing, but I was driven and couldn't quit. I tried not to overdo it when I practiced, and over a period of time my stomach and back muscles became stronger, and the back pain completely disappeared.

As the years have gone by, I find myself dependent on the dance to keep those back muscles strong. I used to take summer breaks from teaching, but by the end of the summer, my back would be trashed and even walking was difficult without pain. I consulted chiropractic and medical doctors, and I was told that my injury had stretched the ligaments in my back to the point of having no elasticity, and that the strength of my back muscles is what was keeping my back in place and pain free. So, now the dance is a constant in my life.

Dance is a physical action, a great exercise; it's no wonder that my body became firm and more toned. When I first started lessons, I fell in love with the dance and practiced several hours a day. I had always suffered from a weight problem, and needed to exercise, but I didn't do it because I hated exercise. Belly dancing was hard work, but it was fun, something I enjoyed doing, and the hours would just fly by, and all the while I was working out. Exercise was boring. Exercise is still boring. I am amazed at my friends who are disciplined enough to spend hours a week doing boring exercises like pushups and sit ups to stay fit. I had found a form of exercise that was fun, and as it turned out was the second best exercise for total body fitness, second only to swimming.

While I got physically fit, a good bonus, another benefit soon became evident.

One day, I was standing in class and doing a rib circle. This is a movement where you actually circle your rib cage. It was a very difficult move for me, and that day, somehow I let go and let it happen. I immediately felt an emotional response and a deep connection with my feminine self.

It is hard to describe the feeling in words as it was an emotional experience unlike any I had ever felt, but somehow I knew that I had become in touch with a part of myself that I had turned my back on, or perhaps never realized was there to begin with. The feeling was wonderful like finding a part of myself that had been lost, but it was also uncomfortable, a feeling of exposure and vulnerability. This was something I knew I needed to look at further.

As a child, I was the oldest of four girls. My father wanted a boy more than anything, and he made it very clear how disappointed he was that he didn't get a boy. In fact, when my third little sister was born, my mom wasn't even allowed to pick a possible girl name during her pregnancy. I remember my dad driving me and my two sisters to the hospital to see our new baby sister and telling us we needed to pick a name for her.

During childhood, I tried everything I could to get my father's attention, approval and acceptance, but that just wasn't going to happen. His rejection created a deep and lasting pain. I grew up thinking, "If only I were a boy, my father would love me." Of course that was a child's rationalization and explanation for the lack of parental love, not reality.

I hated being a girl, and I was sure my life would be better if I'd been a boy, and while I did my best to be as boy-like as possible to win my father's love, I was at the same time rejecting my own femininity.

Then, at age 9, Mother Nature snuck up and blindsided me. I began to grow breasts, and I started my period. I wanted to be a boy, and here I was developing before anyone else I knew. None of my friends had to wear bras. None of my friends dealt with bleeding. It was horrible, horrifying and devastating. Now, I really, really hated being a girl! It sucked big time.

I was already incredibly shy, so wearing bras did nothing to help that as the boys would run up and snap my straps and yell unpleasant things, running away laughing. Not only did I hate being a girl, now I hated boys. My life was poop! Depression became a familiar companion at an early age.

As the years went by, I would walk between classes with books clutched to my chest to cover those unwelcome body attachments. I had very poor posture, hunching forward as if I could somehow make them disappear. I was also incredibly self-conscious about the rest of my body because of being overweight.

My first foray into appreciating being female was pregnancy. As my daughter, Avena, grew inside of me, and I could feel her moving, I felt like I was part of an amazing miracle. Finally, a good reason to be a woman! I was experiencing something that I would never have been able to experience had I been born a man, and it was incredible. I actually felt sorry for her dad, that he would never be able to experience such wonder. I rejoiced in my ability to give life to a new being. I reveled in my woman-ness, but after her birth, I quickly lost touch with that aspect of myself.

When I started dance classes my body was stiff and board-like. Belly dancing is a dance of isolation, and I was like a block of timber with no flexibility. The good news is that I could do head slides, a movement where you slide your head back and forth over your shoulders, making it look like it's disconnected. At least there was one isolation I could do which was a start. The bad news is I couldn't do a hip or shoulder shimmy to save my life. My whole torso was tight and unyielding. When one thing moved, the rest moved with it. Can you say, awkward?

Then, when Avena was four, the rib circle happened. I was standing in class, and I connected with myself. I felt my first inkling of empowerment as I felt my own femininity. It was good, very good to be a woman. Here I was standing straight, my spine in alignment, with no more slouching, and I was moving my rib cage in a circle which meant moving my breasts in a circle since they are attached to the front of my rib cage, and IT FELT GOOD. It felt natural and whole and healing.

Now, I have to say that it wasn't an instant fix, but more like a window into what could be, a glimpse into the depths of the core of my feminine essence.

It was two years before I could do a rib circle in front of an audience because it was hard to overcome my extreme conditioning of shyness and self-consciousness. But, being able to do it in class and in the privacy of my own home was a start.

My next awakening came in the shower. I was taking my daily shower, and of course my thoughts went to the dance. I was thinking about shoulder shimmies, and the next thing I knew, I was doing one right there in the shower. I squealed with delight. I wanted to yell from a mountain top! "Woo hoo! I can do it!"

Bam! Another connection was made. I could do a shoulder shimmy! I could move my shoulders quickly, independent of the rest of my body, isolation and another thing that involved my breasts since they also moved when my shoulders moved. I was elated and even euphoric. It might not sound like much, but for me, it was a huge breakthrough!

It was then that I realized that my body stiffness had more to do with my mind then my body. One second I couldn't do it, and the next second, I could do it. It was a mental limitation, not a physical one, and to this day I try to explain that to my students. I had worked for six months trying to do a shoulder shimmy, and for six months I couldn't do it at all! Then, one day in the shower, it just happened. My body could do it all along. It wasn't a body thing at all, but a mind thing. For whatever reason, I had a mental block against moving that part of my body in that way. It could have to do with my early inhibitions, my upbringing of nice girls don't do that; I don't know for sure, but what I do know is that NOW I COULD DO IT!! I wanted to do it, and it felt good to do it. I felt like celebrating!

Then, there were my hips. Boy, what a challenge! But once I made the shoulder shimmy breakthrough and realized it wasn't a physical limitation, things started to get easier. My hips held my pelvis, the seat of my feminine organs, another problem area. Childhood sexual abuse had left its mark, and I was even shyer from the waist down, then the waist up if such a thing was possible.

As belly dancers, we use our hips and pelvis a lot. We do shimmies and hip points, circles and figure eights. My hips were stiff, but it wasn't long before they began to flow, to move smoothly and freely, and it felt good, still feels good; in fact it feels great!

The hips cradle the pelvis, the power place of women. In the past, women were worshipped for their ability to create and nourish life. In the present, it has often become a place of shame and pain. Belly dancing helps women reclaim their power. It gives women themselves back.

After the rib and chest release, I started learning at what seemed like warp speed, and it was great!

For the first time it felt good to be a woman, felt good to live in a female body. I started to love my body, my breasts, my hips, limbs, and even my face. For the very first time I looked in the mirror and had a brief second of thinking "I'm pretty." And, I didn't just begin to love my body, I loved me, who I was and what I was, extra weight and all.

3 SENSUALITY

After spending my first 23 years hardly even looking into a mirror, and feeling totally unhappy with my physical body, a fat and female body, I start belly dancing and began looking in the mirror a lot!

At first I looked in the mirror to watch my hand and arm movements to see if they were moving evenly. My right arm could do things my left arm couldn't do, and the mirror helped me train my left arm to do the movements correctly. I also watched my head slides, my rib circles and my hips.

First I just watched my movements, looking at the particular body part involved, and then I began to see myself. I watched my hands, and then I saw my hands, not just in the mirror, but I looked at my hands. My hands were small and graceful, and they were actually pretty. My arms were muscular and strong, yet soft and feminine. I had an hourglass figure, and nice womanly hips. For the first time, I really saw 'me,' not just my imagined image of an unattractive blob of flesh, but what I really looked like. I was a woman with full breasts, full hips, very proportioned and even my face wasn't so bad.

Getting in touch with my womanhood was profound and brought me increased awareness about myself. Getting in touch with my sensuality was another story all together.

When I was a younger dancer, I almost quit dancing after only a couple of years. I was told that I was sexy when I danced, and it totally freaked me out.

I didn't want to be sexy. Sex was the last thing on my mind when I danced. Dancing was my passion, my joy, my release, my escape. It had nothing to do with sex. Dance was pure, but sex wasn't, and I hated to hear the word sexy associated with what I did.

I almost quit, but I didn't. I knew I'd hit another obstacle in my personal growth, and I needed to work through it. I needed to look at why this bothered me so much and get over it.

It took me years to work this one through which is no surprise, being a survivor of childhood sexual abuse.

What I discovered was my sensuality. Despite the abuse, I felt that I was in touch with my sexuality, and I loved having sex. That was a totally separate issue from my dance. And, over time I realized that sex was pure, after all, and that it was people who made it something impure.

Sensuality was something new. I had spent years, shutting down my senses. As a child I would feel something was wrong, and was told there was nothing wrong. When I saw things that weren't right in my family I was told I didn't see anything. When I heard angry voices behind closed doors, I was told I didn't hear anything, that everything was fine. And, good touching and hugging weren't part of my life, but beatings and molestation were. By the time I left home, I was pretty much shut down sensually, and I had to learn how to touch, listen, see and most of all how to feel.

So, here I was drawn to a very sensual, very feminine art form, the perfect avenue for opening up my sensuality.

At first I just danced, and when someone made a remark that I was sexy, I just denied it in my mind. I wasn't sexy, they just imagined it. I didn't do anything wrong, they just thought I did. These were my rationalizations, and they kept me performing until I could process things.

Believe it or not, it was a drunken stranger that helped me become more aware. My girlfriends and I went out to a lounge, the only thing open after our dance show was over. We didn't want the evening to end, and we sat around talking and laughing over our Pepsi. None of us were drinking alcohol, just hanging out. A man that one of my friends knew came over and sat down with us. He sat next to me and was very drunk. He reached out and very gently touched my hair and said, "You're very beautiful." My friend, Tammy said, "Oh, Larry, you're just drunk." He said, "I may be drunk, but she's still beautiful."

It was like a light bulb went off in my head. I suddenly understood that I was me, a sexual being either on or off the stage, that it had nothing at all to do with my dance. If someone thought I was beautiful or sexy, they were going to think that when I walked down the street or when I was sitting in a restaurant or dancing on a stage. It wasn't my dancing that they thought was sexy, it was me they thought was sexy so whether I walked, sat or danced, what I did was in their mind sexy.

Wow, that took a burden off of my brain. My dance wasn't sexy; it was me who was perceived as being sexy. So, what did that mean? Wasn't that bad too? I put that one on the shelf for awhile until I had counseling which helped me accept myself, sexy or otherwise.

So, how does this pertain to my dance? To me and all dancers I've talked to, it's okay to dance sensually, but it's not okay to dance sexually.

This is an extremely important issue to most belly dancers, and after giving this a lot of thought, I brought it to my Monday night class which is my advanced class. I told my students that I needed their help with this chapter, and it turned into one of the most fun and funny classes ever.

First we talked about sensual versus sexual. Sensual is soft, subtle and illusory. Sexual is hard, obvious and in your face. It's all about energy with sensual being a more inner process and sexual being an outer process. Sensual is, "I'm here to entertain and delight you." Sexual dancing is, "I'm here to turn you on."

When we dance sensually, we are fully in our bodies. We are more aware of our movements and of how we physically feel as we do them. We are listening to the music and to what the music is telling us to express and allowing our movements to flow with the music. We are looking at our audience and allowing our personal expression, our own special essences to project to them. We see them, see their eyes, their body posture and we become part of them. This is sensual, feeling, hearing, seeing, sharing and connecting with our audience on an inner level, giving them something to see, hear and feel on a deeper level as they watch us.

Women who dance sexually also connect with their audience, but in a very different way, a superficial way. As an audience member, myself, when a dancer is sexual; I am uncomfortable. I don't feel a connection with the dancer like I do with a sensual dancer. If she is a belly dancer,

I'm also appalled and angered because she is desecrating my beautiful art form.

Fortunately, very, very few belly dancers I've seen dance sexually. And, from what I've seen, it seems like they are trying to get attention more than anything. For instance, I've seen a couple of older dancers start dancing more sexually as they aged as if they were afraid they were losing their allure and had to add sexual moves so people would remember them. I've also seen a couple of dancers get drunk and get stupid. One dancer was in street clothes at a Middle Eastern night club where I had a dance gig. She became very drunk and then during open dance got up on the stage and started dancing and rubbing her breasts and lifting her mini skirt and touching her crotch while gyrating. I was horrified, disgusted and angry, not to mention embarrassed.

I once saw a dance production at a major festival where belly dancers were purposely enacting Kama Sutra moves as part of their performance. (Now what the Kama Sutra (from India) has to do with belly dance (from the Middle East) is a mystery to all of us.) They also simulated these acts with black men who acted as their slaves. Their sexual movements and sexual acting were inappropriate, but the venue being a family festival made their routine outrageous as parents rushed out of the building with little ones in tow.

I'm not sure what they were or weren't thinking; I just know what I thought. I thought they were desperate for attention, desperate to stand out from the rest of the dancers. What made it extra sad is that these ladies were excellent dancers, but obviously didn't believe in their abilities to stand out with their talent alone and had to go to the extreme to be noticed and remembered. They were noticed, and they were remembered, but not for their beautiful abilities as belly dancers.

Their argument was that what they did was innovative, and they say that their artistic freedom was being compromised when people objected to their performance. I say that in an after-hours night club in Vegas, I might have appreciated their artistic expression, but on a stage at a family event, explicit sex act simulation, including oral and even anal sex was very inappropriate. Then there was the issue of slavery simulation in their act which also offended many people. How anyone can defend what they did in that venue is something that goes beyond my ability to understand. Belly dancers have fought for years to overcome the stigmas that have been placed on us. Unless this group landed here recently from outer space, they had to know that what they were doing was offensive and inappropriate, but chose to do it anyway.

Those are my memories of sexual dancers and dancing, not bad really out of the thousands of performances I've seen. But, this is what we have been fighting against for decades. As belly dancers, we educate the public constantly that what we do is family entertainment, not stripping. Along comes a dancer or dancers like this and it sets us back, and we have to fight even harder for legitimacy.

As women, we might be sexy, but our dance is not sexy. The roots of our dance are feminine; it's mainly a feminine expression and the costuming emphasizes the female figure. A typical cabaret costume has a beaded or coin bra and belt over skirt and harem pants. This emphasizes the breast and hips, two of the most feminine parts of our bodies. There are also jewelry and hair adornments. Even though the costume might emphasize our lady parts, they are not on display as something sexual. There is a huge difference between being sexy and dancing sexually.

Most dancers would agree that it's okay to be playful and flirty, and okay to have fun with our audience but not inappropriately. For instance, a 'big name' dancer in the business, once stopped her dancing, looked down and grabbed her breasts, and moved them like she was re-adjusting them. What she did was 'sexy,' but her intent was to be funny, not sexual, and the audience roared with laughter. I can't help but wonder if she really wanted to be remembered by her audience as the dancer who grabbed her boobs instead of as a great belly dancer?

So, I asked my students, what are some examples of sensual moves versus sexual moves, and the fun began. One movement we do is called a Turkish pelvic drop. It's done by squeezing the gluteus muscles then relaxing them which tucks the pelvis, then releases it looking like a drop. When done incorrectly, instead of tucking the pelvis, some dancers thrust it forward and then drop it. This looks sexual, like something you do in bed, not in a belly dance performance. Sometimes the dancer does this with intent, and sometimes, she just had a bad teacher who either taught the move incorrectly or who didn't notice that she was doing it wrong and correct her.

Another move is the shoulder shimmy. This is done with the spine straight, arms out and moving the shoulders forward and back in small fast movements. When I teach it, I emphasize being dignified while doing it. It's a very empowering move when done correctly. When dancers lean forward to do a shoulder shimmy, it becomes a boob shimmy, and is sexual as the breasts swing back and forth.

Each of my students took a turn showing the rest of us the difference between sensual moves and sexual moves.

When, Aluma, my home-schooled seemingly innocent, teenaged student did a boob shimmy in another student's face to demonstrate a 'sexual' move, we all just about fell on the floor.

Kateena, our fun loving microbiologist by day, showed us how touching ourselves while belly dancing can turn what we are doing into something pretty nasty. Oh my!!

Miranda is our very proper English teacher, and she showed us how lifting our hair when we dance can be very sensual, or very sexual. Then she did some things with the veil that made us all blush.

Our sexy senior, Lateesha, demonstrated how the mere act of tasting a strawberry can look extremely sexual.

So, the subject matter is very serious especially for those of us who have worked so hard to overcome the stigma of misinformation. But, when we get together with just us women, we can make fun and have fun with the whole idea of sexuality.

That night, my studio was filled with laughter, but we all agreed that we are dancers expressing the beauty of the music with our movements, dressed in beautiful costumes also expressing our own unique individuality, and it has nothing at all to do with sex. It's all about the dance! It's a dance that can be sensual, feminine, dramatic, saucy and fun. Some may argue with me, but in my opinion, the dance is not sexual. It is something very separate, and for me personally, the dance is something sacred.

4 CONFIDENCE

Another thing belly dancing gave me is confidence and self-esteem. Learning to like my body was helpful for my self-esteem, and connecting with my own femininity was great, and a step toward healing inner wounds, but my biggest obstacle, and I believe, everyone's biggest obstacles are overcoming fears. I lived in a world of fear. What is shyness but the fear of talking to people? What is self-consciousness but the fear of being judged and found lacking?

It was one thing to learn to dance, learn to move my body in new ways, and learn to connect with myself as a woman and all that good stuff. It was another thing to PERFORM!

Yikes! The very thought of it sent my stomach to my throat and my heart to beating at warp speed. At first, my mantra was "I'll never perform, ever!" But, I liked how the dance was making me feel. I liked liking myself. I liked overcoming personal obstacles. I liked the personal growth I was experiencing. And, I still hated being so very shy and self-conscious.

So, here was a perfect growth opportunity. Just make up a dance and do it in front of other people. That will get you out of your shell!

Yeah, right. Just get up and dance.

Well, I really did hate being so shy, and I really wanted to get over it, so I forced myself to perform.

This is how it came down. First of all, I made a costume which was the easy part, since I already sewed and beaded and all that creative stuff. Then, I had to have a dance. I picked out some music, and spent hours, and I mean hours making up choreography. Next, I practiced the dance hundreds of times at least. It became an automatic body response, a cellular memory where my mind could just shut off and my body would still know the dance. I swear, I could do it in my sleep. I completely memorized each movement and each nuance of each movement. I choreographed down to my finger tips; even the tiniest detail was choreographed including practicing smiling.

Next was the performance itself.

I told my teacher I had a dance made up, and she asked me to perform it for her new beginner class. There I was in the dance studio I was familiar with, and I was terrified, almost paralyzed with fear. It took every speck of my self-resolve to force myself to do the dance. I was standing there in front of a few friendly-looking faces; my teacher started the music, and I started to dance. I don't remember much except my terror, but I got through it and everyone CLAPPED! Wow, what nice people, I thought; they are just being nice and polite.

My first dance performing for my class.

Afterwards, one student told me, "That's the best dance I've ever seen!" It wasn't until years later when she was my own student that I overheard her tell person after person "That's the best dance I've ever seen!" and I realized that was just her way of giving someone a compliment and that every dance is the best she's ever seen. But, at the time, it meant everything to me and really gave me a boost.

Another dancer told me she had never seen vibrating snake arms before, that it was the most advanced dance movement she'd ever seen and she wondered how did I do it? I told her, it was called 'terror.' When you are that terrified, you shake so hard, it looks like you are vibrating. This is a story I've shared with all of my students who are afraid to perform.

So, what did I learn from this? I learned that even in complete mind-melting terror you can impress people and that despite that terror; I wanted to hear that applause again.

I was officially hooked!

A couple of weeks later, we had company in our home, and my daughter said, "Mommy, put on your belly dance music." So I put on some belly dance music. "No, your music," she insisted. It took me a minute, but then I realized she meant the music for my dance I had choreographed. I put it on, and she did my dance exactly, and she did it better than me. I was astounded. She had never shown the slightest interest in what I was doing, and I'd never even noticed her watching me, but there she was doing my dance perfectly. I was, of course, a thrilled and proud mom and took her to class with me the very next week to show my teacher.

Well, Kadriyah was also impressed and she asked if Avena could dance in her next show. Unlike me, Avena didn't have a shy bone in her body, so she was happy to dance anywhere. I made her a costume, put some tiny braids in her long hair, and she had her public performance debut before I did. There she was on the stage, a whole four years old, a tiny little thing dancing her heart out and melting the hearts of everyone in the audience. I was so proud, and felt so much joy; I didn't think I could stand the excitement of it.

While she stole our hearts, she also gave us all a laugh. The dance ended with a spin and a bow, and when her spin stopped she was facing the back of the stage, and that's when she bowed giving us a great view of her little backside. She was so precious and cute. The bow was just part of the dance to her, and she had no awareness that a bow was for the audience. So everyone was clapping, cheering and chuckling all at the same time.

My daughter, Avena, age 4 performing in a show.

It wasn't very long before my teacher also asked me to perform. She had a dance gig and asked me to do my dance while she did a quick costume change. I was scared stiff, but eager to do it, another growth experience. This time I was dancing on a stage in a theatre with stage lights.

While it was probably good for my first real performance, it's my least favorite venue, even now. The reason I don't like this venue is that the stage lights are so bright; you can't see your audience which was a plus for me when I was so terrified. All I saw was blinding white light, so I pretended I was in my own living room dancing.

The next time I danced was at a coffee house, and again, I was terrified. This time we danced up close and personal to the audience. I was sure it would be a disastrous experience, but the music started, and I danced into the room. I'll never forget that experience. I was so afraid to be that close to people. What was I afraid of? I really don't know. I guess it was that shy thing again. What happened? Since it was a close and personal experience with no bright stage lights in my eyes, I could see their eyes, and their lips which were mostly smiling. Then, there were their hands which were clapping along with the music and it felt like support.

My first dance was three minutes long and on stage under the bright lights, it felt like an hour. In the restaurant, the same dance felt like 30 seconds. I loved dancing close to the people, loved watching their expressions as they watched me and really loved feeling their appreciation. We were having fun *together*, and for the first time I felt the rush that I later learned was my endorphins flowing. It was a natural high, and I immediately became an addict.

The week of my first lesson, I attended a belly dance competition with my friend Ishtar. We had a great time choosing who we thought would win each category. I pegged them all except one, a dancer who literally oozed emotion. Little did I know that I would meet her soon, and our lives would connect on a deep level.

After my first couple of dance experiences, I was encouraged by my teacher to enter the next competition. My first reaction was, no way, Jose! I'm not competitive, and I wasn't about to get on that stage with judges sitting there with their clip boards and score sheets. I just wasn't ready!

But, of course, here was another opportunity for a growth experience, and I convinced myself that it was one that I needed and immediately started preparing.

First and foremost was the hunt for new music. Then I started designing a new costume. My biggest challenge was learning to play the zills. These are mini finger cymbals.

I found the music I wanted and again spent hours and hours doing choreography. No one taught me how to do this, and I just used common sense. I had a certain vocabulary of dance movements. First I started with my entrance, and where my weight was placed at the end of the entrance is where I started my next movement so each would flow into the next.

Zills were a requirement in the competition, and they were a huge challenge. I discovered that I didn't have any natural rhythm, and danced mostly to the melody. Fortunately, a dumbek workshop was offered in our town, and I eagerly attended it. I learned the most common Middle Eastern rhythm, Beladi, and practiced and practiced. I didn't have a drum, so I practiced on my thighs, counter tops and kitchen tables. Doom Doom, Tek Ka Tek, Doom Tek Ka Tek, Tek Ka! Over and over, and before long I began to feel the rhythm, and even hear it.

After that, I was able to play the zills. As it turns out, that was the easy part! Yikes! Now I had to zill *and* dance. Ballet dancers have a tendency to look down on us mere belly dancers. I know that their art form takes years of practice and even foot deformities, but boy would I like to see them play a musical instrument while they dance before they belittle my beloved art form.

So, hours and hours of practice later, I realized that dancing and zilling wasn't going to happen in time for the contest. I fussed and worried and strained my brain and finally, it hit me. I would just zill during part of my dance. I could only do three steps while zilling, Egyptian walk, Persian walk and the Egyptian spin, and hoped the judges wouldn't know that.

My new costume was the easy part. I bought some emerald green satin and made a full circular skirt and Turkish vest edged with gold metallic trim. I made a bra and belt with gold coins, cream harem pants and a sheer cream veil trimmed with green sequins.

The contest quickly approached, and I became a total basket case. My nerves were continually on edge. I practiced hours a day and dreaded getting on that stage. I have to say that the closer it got, the less fun it all became, and I began to regret choosing this particular growth experience, as did my poor family.

When the day came, I found out that I wasn't the only one in terror. Being in the beginner category, I performed early which was great with me. I needed to get it over with before I imploded. Back stage in the dressing room, I found that other newbies were just as scared as I was, with one even vomiting with fear. We were all in this together and supporting each other which helped a bit to take the edge off.

When they announced me and started my music, I think I was almost in a trance. I remember going through the motions, and I vaguely remember looking down from the raised stage into a sea of faces. I kept telling myself to just smile, and I felt like my grin was permanently fixed on my face like the Cheshire cat. While I danced, I felt great, but when my music stopped, the audience applauded, and my terror returned. I almost ran off of the stage.

I was too nervous to watch the other dancers in my category, and found myself shopping at the vendor tables. I had never seen so much splendorous goods in my life, beautiful fabrics, jewelry, music and goo gahs.

While I was shopping, a man grabbed me and said "It's you! It's you!" I was totally freaked out and tried to pull away, but he finally got through to me. "They are calling your name!"

I looked up at the stage, and found a room full of people looking at me expectantly. As it turns out, I won second place! While I was thrilled that I had won, I now had to go up on stage and accept the award. For some reason that was even more frightening then dancing. What I later realized was that while I was dancing, I felt like a different person, whereas it was just me accepting the award. There began a longer road of personal change.

Winning second place in that competition was the start towards building my self-confidence. For the first time I was acknowledged for doing something well. I had worked extremely hard, and I had been rewarded. I not only received attention, but more importantly, acceptance.

My first competition.

The hook went even deeper!

I continued to take classes, I performed any chance I could get, and my confidence grew. One performance venue was night clubs. I traveled over four hours to dance in clubs in Portland, and I had a great time. Sometimes I danced to taped music, and sometimes to live music. The Arabic clubs were my favorite. It didn't matter that I was overweight, or non-Arabic, it only mattered that I danced. I received lots of compliments, mostly about my dancing and how I expressed as an Arabic woman would when I danced. I had dollars and larger bills folded and tucked into my belt and it was like dancing in another world.

I was also hit on by Arabic men which was very different then being hit on by American men. Arabic men are flowery speakers and act very respectful and decent towards women, at first.

When an Arabic man hit on me, he would say something such as: "My heart is filled with joy when I look into your beautiful eyes. Your lips are like the sweetest nectarines kissed by the warmth of the sun, and your hair is soft as a gentle breeze on the beach of the red sea under the moonlight. Please give me the great honor of buying you a drink."

Can you say, 'swoon?'

When I said I was married, Arabic men respected that, and they never crossed that boundary or even suggested they might. American men weren't as respectful.

However, I learned very early that Arabic men weren't the best marriage material for women raised in America. The cultural differences are difficult barriers to overcome, and the expectations of Arabic men are very different than the ones of American men. First and foremost, dancing comes to an end after marrying an Arabic man, and if people think our culture is patriarchal, it pales in comparison to Arabic cultures.

But, I just wanted to dance and have fun. The clubs were great for my self-esteem, and the tips were plentiful. Sometimes I was showered with money, and sometimes long necklaces of bills stapled or taped together were draped around me as I danced. It was an experience I will always treasure and one that helped me come even further out of my shell.

5 HEALING

One day, my dance partner, Saheena and I were at a competition where we were entering as a duet in the intermediate category. At the time there were only solo categories, no duet or troupe categories. As far as I know, we were the first to enter a competition as a duet at least in the Northwest.

In the dressing room, Saheena complained that her hip was hurting, and a dancer named Leanne overheard her and came over to us. She said, "I know a healing method called Reiki, where I put my hands on you to help the pain go away. Would you like me to do it?" Saheena was open to it, so Leanne put her hands on her hip and held them there. Saheena said she could feel the warmth from her hands, and that it was helping the pain.

As I watched her, I was immediately intrigued and wanted to learn more. I had always felt a sensation in my own hands, and felt like there was something I was supposed to do but didn't have a clue what it might be. This method called me very strongly. As soon as I heard about it, I was determined to learn how to do it.

I asked Leanne question after question. How did it work? Where did she learn it? How could I learn it? She was very patient, but vague. She gave me the name and phone number of her teacher, and suggested I call her.

Saheena and I danced in the competition, and we got 2nd place. Competing wasn't near as frightening this time since we were in it together. As a duet, we danced very well together, each of us with a different strength and helping each other develop what we didn't personally have. Undulations and graceful arms were my forte, and fiery shimmies were Saheena's best asset. Together we were a great blend of fire and water and got a lot of positive attention.

As soon as we got home from the competition, I called the number Leanne had given me and spoke for the first time to Marta, a Reiki Master. She told me she had a class set up in Portland the following weekend, and I immediately registered over the phone. She gave me the times and address, and I called my belly dance friend Halima to see if I could stay with her while I took the class. She was happy to have me.

When Friday came, I drove up to Portland to Halima's house and asked her husband Bud for directions to the class. Despite his good directions, I got lost and arrived about 20 minutes late. Still feeling shy in new situations, I felt embarrassed as I walked into a stranger's living room filled with 12 students listening intently to Marta speak about Reiki. I apologized for being late, but no one seemed to have an issue with it, and I was warmly welcomed.

That evening, Marta was giving an introductory talk about Reiki, explaining that it was a hands-on form of healing where the practitioner allowed Universal Life Energy to flow through their hands and into the person receiving the healing. She explained how unlike other forms of healing where the practitioner uses her own energy or takes on pain or symptoms from the patient, Reiki was one-directional. The energy flows through the practitioner, through the patient and back out to the universe. While channeling the energy, the practitioner receives any healing energy she or he may need as it passes through.

Marta also shared the history of Reiki and gave a demonstration, showing how the practitioner gently lays her hands on the person receiving and explaining that Reiki can be given any time and any place. A quiet room with soft music flowing is the ideal situation for healing work, but it works equally well anywhere and can be used in emergency situations to help with pain relief.

Reiki works on all levels, physical, mental, emotional and spiritual. The practitioner makes no judgment calls, but rather just allows the energy to flow and trusts that it goes where needed.

This aspect really appealed to me. I didn't believe that I knew what was best for anyone else, but I did want to help people, and Reiki seemed a great way to do this.

As the weekend progressed, Marta taught us the hand positions for a Reiki treatment. She talked about how people could feel the energy flow in different ways, as heat, tingling or other sensation, and she gave us a lot of information about the emotional aspects of physical ailments. It was a real eye opener for me as well as validation.

For instance, she said that the liver stores anger, and when it becomes too intense, it spills out into the gall bladder as bitterness. Since my childhood totally sucked, I was a very angry teen. By the age of 20, I had gall bladder disease usually a disease that appears after the age of 40. After surgery at age 21, I was told that I had some of the largest gall stones the surgeon had ever seen. I couldn't help but wonder if I'd known the effects my emotions could have if I could have avoided surgery by letting go of my anger and bitterness before they manifested into gall bladder disease.

Learning Reiki was a life-changing event. I had always believed that emotions caused illness, and here my belief was being validated. Now we have scientific proof that stress and emotion cause illness, but at that time it was a just an unsubstantiated belief that I didn't know anyone else shared.

I immediately started using Reiki on myself and my family, but I couldn't feel any energy sensations and didn't know if it was working. I contacted Marta and set up a meeting with her because I was so concerned. I totally believed that Reiki worked, but I didn't believe that it was working for me.

First of all, Marta reassured me that it worked for anyone and everyone whether we felt it working or not. She then asked me if I had ever worked on anyone really sick, and I told her no, just myself and my family members. She suggested that I try working on someone who was actually ill and see if I felt anything happening.

I had a belly dance student with advanced cancer, and I called and asked her if I could give her some Reiki. It turned out to be a very intense experience. After putting my hands on her, I could feel a strong tingling sensation as well as heat. My hands started to feel extremely hot, and she told me that it felt uncomfortable, too hot, so I lifted my hands off of her and just kept them in her energy field. It definitely gave me a new awareness, and it brought me much closer to my friend.

A month later I took the second level of Reiki. In this class, we learned various symbols that helped direct the energy, help with mental clarity and how to send it long distance.

I have always been a high-energy, high-stressed person. I was also on guard all the time, because of what I now know as PTSD. I didn't know what relaxation felt like. I tried many visualization and relaxation methods, and none of them worked. I couldn't let go. I first felt relaxation during a Reiki treatment and it was pure heaven. While receiving the treatment, I totally let go and relaxed. It was the first time I went to what I call La La Land, and let me tell you, that is a wonderful place. After feeling what relaxed felt like, I was finally able to relax at will, a great tool to have.

For myself, I'd had infertility problems and other pelvic problems. I had to take fertility drugs to become pregnant with my daughter, and after her birth had more problems. At one point, I was told by my obstetrician that my ovaries were necrotized and that I would never be able to have another child. I mourned not being able to have more children but was very grateful for my beautiful daughter. About a year after learning Reiki, I began to have severe pelvic pain and went to the Dr. to see what was going on. An ultrasound, showed that I had developed two very large cysts, one on each ovary. I was told that they were the type of cysts that wouldn't go away without surgery. When I refused to have surgery, my doctor told me that I would be back when my quality of life suffered enough.

I had other ideas and went to two of my friends, Jim and Ann DeSmet who did Reiki. They gave me a treatment, and we talked about possible emotional issues that might be causing this problem. The pain began to recede and a few weeks later, an ultrasound showed no sign of the cysts.

Because my pelvis was filled with health issues, I would go to sleep giving myself Reiki with my hands on my lower abdomen. My intent was to give a problem area healing. After a few years, I woke up one day and felt like I had gotten pregnant the night before. I told myself I was imagining things, but it turned out that I had conceived my son that night. He was and is a blessing in my life, a gift of Reiki.

Before I learned Reiki, I had horrible stage fright. Every time I danced, I got so stressed out before the performance that I snapped and growled and was incredibly tense for days preceding the event. My husband asked me how I could love something so much that made me so crazy with stress. After Reiki, I started using the symbols and energy before events and back stage, and I immediately felt calm and relaxed. Stage fright was no longer an issue.

One powerful aspect of the dance is stage presence and personal expression. Every dancer has this to some degree, some more than others. This is how the dancer reaches her audience. Some dancers are remote, unable or unwilling to give of themselves, but I have always been a dancer who gives. After Reiki, that also changed and became profound. Over time, I began to feel energy flow through me more and more strongly as I performed and flowing out to my audience. I often go into an altered state when I dance and have no memory of what I did during my performance. When this happens, I am totally able to let go and just allow the music to flow through me and allow my body to express the music without my analytical mind telling it what to do. It is a completely creative state, and what I feel can only be described as bliss.

I have had all kinds of feedback over the years regarding my dance. Some people see light emanating from my hands as I dance, some of them feeling the healing energy.

One day after a performance, my husband asked me, "How do you do that thing you do when you dance?" I asked him what thing?" I thought he was referring to some movement or dance step I was doing, but I was way off base. "That thing where you fill the whole room with love," he told me.

I was so touched. He got it. He really got it. While I dance, I don't just feel energy flow through me and out to the audience, I feel that energy as pure unconditional love flowing from my heart out through my arms and out my hands. It's not me 'doing it,' but a beautiful energy channeling through me. Sometimes it's actually overwhelming to me. I feel that the amount that comes through is sometimes stronger due to the needs of the people watching. Sometimes I feel pulled off the stage and go directly into the audience and dance giving personal attention to various audience members.

Once at Belly Dancer USA, one of the competitors was very ill and could barely walk. I sat her down and called in the troops. Several of my dance/Reiki students gave her Reiki and not only was she able to dance, but she won!

Belly dancing brought me to Reiki, and Reiki has enhanced my dancing and my entire life. I eventually became a Reiki master. I have received amazing personal healing, and I have witnessed incredible healing miracles as a facilitator for others. I could write a book on Reiki alone.

Another healing method the dance brought to me is Shamanism. I had a dance room in my home at the time, and I had 10 people registered for my next class. All had called and registered over the phone and were going to pay the first night of my class. Another person called and told me she was a channel for what she called 'the teachers' and she wanted to know if she could use my space for a meditation class after my dance class. She said that some of her students might also want to take belly dance lessons. I wasn't sure what I would do with everyone, but welcomed her to come use my space.

The first night of my new dance class, not one of the ten pre-registered students showed up, not even one. But, I had a full class with the students who came for the meditation class. Two of these students ended up being two of my best friends, life-long soul sisters, Gail and Tammy. I taught these ladies to dance, and they taught me Shamanic journeying; once again my life was changed.

Shamanism isn't what I thought it was or what most people think or imagine it is. It sounds strange, people going into an altered state and contacting their spirit guides or power animals, or retrieving lost soul parts or extracting things that are causing personal harm. It sounds weird or alternative or to some evil.

But the reality is that Shamanism is a healing method used by ancient people around the world. It pre-dates modern science, modern medicine and was a way to help people heal their bodies and their spirits.

My experience of Shamanism is that when I travel in my altered state, I access knowledge that isn't available to me in the way that I have learned to experience. Scientists say we only use 10% of our brains, and Shamanism is a way for me to use a part of my brain that isn't normally used in our modern society. But, I believe it is a part of the brain that ancient cultures had access to help them heal.

One of the beliefs of Shamanism is that we all have power animals. Again, this might sound strange, but it isn't really the animal itself; it's the energy that the animal represents. Bear represents a powerful, grounding energy, while humming bird might represent a more detailed, yet quick energy. Getting in touch with our power animals, helps us get in touch with different aspects of ourselves that need our attention.

The most profound use for Shamanism is soul retrieval. The belief is that when a person suffers a trauma such as a physical injury or a loss of a loved one, a part of their soul leaves as a way of coping with the pain. In ancient cultures, when a person suffered such a trauma, the Shaman was called immediately to help retrieve the soul part and help the person become whole again.

When I first heard about soul retrievals, it immediately felt like truth. In fact, there were at least two times in my life where I knew I had suffered soul loss. Once was when I was five years old and molested by a family member. The other time was when my first husband, the love of my life, told me he was in love with another woman. The first time, I remember leaving my body and going somewhere that felt safe; the second time I actually experienced leaving my body and going up in the air where I looked down and saw myself sitting on the stump while my husband spoke to me. It was an actual out-of-body experience caused by shock and trauma. After a moment, I felt myself go back into my body and I was again looking out of my physical eyes, facing my husband, but, I didn't feel the same. I felt like something was missing, but never could express what it was until I heard about soul retrieval.

I asked my friends if they could do a soul retrieval for me, and they immediately agreed. Gail drummed while Tammy and I laid side by, and she journeyed for me. When she was done, she described two soul parts, one from when I was what she described as being a four to six years old, and one from when I looked to be about 30. I immediately felt a shift inside of myself, felt more grounded and whole. It was amazing. Even more amazing was that Tammy had no idea about my past, and yet she hit the two times I had felt soul losses. It was a profound experience for me, and I wanted to learn how to do it myself.

I did learn how to do soul retrievals, and I've seen it help some people and others seem to feel no difference. I'm not sure how it fits in my life; I just know that it had a profound healing impact on me, and I still occasionally journey just for my own benefit and sometimes for the benefit of close friends.

Belly dancing brought me both Reiki and Shamanism, and between the three I have found not only amazing personal growth but also physical and psychological healing. Even better, I have been able to help others with their own healing process.

I feel that I have been truly blessed to have these three healing modalities in my life. I truly love myself. I like who I am. I feel comfortable in my own skin, comfortable in the world and confident of my abilities. Out of the three, belly dancing has had the most direct and profound healing impact in my life.

The reason I feel so blessed is because I can look around me and see people suffering, filled with angst and self-incrimination, self-deprecation.

What I have observed is that the dance helps us overcome shyness and self-consciousness. However, it only helps us heal if we want to be healed. It gives us confidence in groups and a connection to other women, and the alternative healing arts help us heal our deeper demons.

Another profound healing aspect of the dance for me is it gave me a way to cope with my life- long battle with depression.

I used to be depressed to some degree from mild to severe, and have had doctors tell me that I need to be on anti-depressants for the rest of my life. I even had a doctor tell me that my depression was a chemical imbalance and that I could no more cure it without drugs than I could change my blue eyes to brown. Those were his words.

Unfortunately, many doctors just prescribe drugs, and don't suggest counseling or physical exercise such as dance.

My experience is that dancing is better than any drug in the world. When you dance, your brain releases endorphins which are very nice things. Dancing is the greatest high in the world and all natural.

Now, I don't mean just coming to class once a week, but also practicing and performing. In other words, dancing as much as possible helps depression.

That being said, there are different levels of depression and when it becomes severe, it can be disabling and an anti-depressant might be called for. I've taken them briefly three times in my life, and they have helped me keep my head above water and get back on track when I felt like I was drowning in pain.

I've also had counseling which helped give me coping tools, but unless something drastic happens such as death or divorce, the dancing is what keeps my depression away.

It's not just the physical aspect of dancing, and being a dancer, it's also my connection with the dance community, my students and friends.

For instance, when I went through my last divorce I became profoundly depressed, having lost the love of my life, my income, my home and even my car. One night during troupe, I expressed how I was feeling. Of course they knew I was going through a hard time, but that night I couldn't leave it at the door. Their response was total love, compassion and empathy. I have rarely felt more loved and I felt a shift inside and my emotional healing began.

During this time, I wrote an article for *Jareeda* about depression. I struggled with some self-doubts about it. '*Jareeda*' is a belly dance publication, not 'Psychology Today,' and it was deeply personal, outing myself about having a mental illness. But, I put my doubts aside telling myself if it helped even one person, it would be worth printing.

The response was definitely an affirmation for following my guidance. In almost twenty years of publishing '*Jareeda*' and writing for other publications, I have never gotten as much response to anything like I did to my article on depression. I received several emails and phone calls, and people at events still come up and tell me how it helped them or they thank me for writing it.

Each of us has our own unique experience of life; the world would be a much better place if we all just supported each other without judgment. It's important to be there for the people in your life who suffer emotional pain, and if that person is you, be there for yourself. You can do it. I believe in you.

6 COMMUNITY

How can I ever describe what it feels like to be part of such a wonderful community? Community was something I missed as a child. Being 'dysfunctional,' my family stayed isolated. We never knew our cousins, or extended family. We lived on an Apache reservation, and I wasn't allowed to visit my Apache friends or bring them home. We had no culture and no traditions.

My Apache friends had both culture and tradition as well as strong family ties. Working in our trading post I learned so much from our employees. I would ask questions daily. I also rode almost three hours a day on a school bus and longed to have beautiful, long black hair like my friends, and dark brown skin. I know we always want what we don't have, but my blonde hair and pale white skin just couldn't compare in my eyes.

I remember how a woman across the river was barren, so her sister gave her one of her own children to raise. I was amazed at the bond of their family. Once, I found a carved stone charm and some beads on the floor of our trading post. As I leaned down to pick it up, our butcher rushed up and grabbed me and yelled, "No!" Then as everyone was chattering in horror and in Apache which I couldn't understand, he went and got a broom. Holding it by the broom end, he picked up the charm with the end of the handle and gingerly carried it out the door holding it as far away from himself as he could. No one would tell me what that thing was, but it was bad and everyone in that store knew what it meant except me.

Then there was the drumming and chanting of songs that had been passed down through thousands of years. And there were traditions such as the coming-out ceremony for girls when they started their periods, a week-long celebration of dancing and give-aways as the girl passed from childhood into becoming a woman. They are a matriarchal society, which made total sense to me.

I knew the Apaches had something I wanted, but I couldn't exactly put my finger on it. Growing up, I craved something; knew I was missing something, but really didn't know what it was until I had it.

What I missed as a child was a sense of community. Belly dancing gave me that community, and it also gave me culture.

Some people call it a sisterhood, and that is a good description since 99% of belly dancers are women. We do have a sisterhood, but it goes beyond that.

Since I was raised in such an isolated way, I never really had close friends. My first husband and I moved to a piece of land in Oregon surrounded by thousands of acres of BLM land. Again, I was isolated, this time even more than before.

Belly dancing brought me friends. My first friend was, Ishtar, the neighbor I first went to class with. We had fun practicing together, and we soon met Saheena who later became my dance partner, and another dancer named Marissa. We decided to make up a dance together and got together on a regular basis to practice. We learned a lot of new steps from Marissa who took week-long workshops from Jamilla Salimpour in San Francisco.

Our first dance was done to a song called 'Mastoum, Mastoum,' and our only performance was for our class. I'll never forget how I felt something creep up to my waist thinking it was my skirt and later discovering it was my white granny panties! Next we did a dance of the Ouled Nail that Marissa taught us, and we were asked to perform as guest dancers at the competition where I had won my first trophy. The Ouled Nail were a tribe in the Middle East who wore lots of fabric draped around themselves, elaborate head pieces and lots of jewelry to display their wealth. Ishtar was so scared that she threw up right before we performed and she seemed to be in a trance during the whole dance. Despite that, we did well with no mistakes and that was my start with troupe dancing.

As time went by, both Ishtar and Marissa dropped out of the dance, and Saheena and I kept going. We started teaching classes together, and we danced as a duet. She was fire, and I was water, so we complimented each other. During classes, she taught shimmies, and I taught undulations, and we had a lot of fun traveling and meeting other dancers.

Saheena and I started bringing in teachers from out of town. One dancer was named, Jeena, and she was my greatest dance inspiration. There was a time when I almost quit dancing. I felt too big, awkward and unappreciated. All of the dancers around me were fast and fiery, and I was slow and fluid and I often felt very out of place.

During Jeena's first workshop, I was totally mesmerized by her movements. She was all feminine grace literally flowing with each step she took. After her workshop, she took me aside and asked me if I was a water sign. I told her I didn't know what that meant, and she explained that there were water, earth, air and fire signs. Scorpio, Cancer and Pisces were water signs.

It turned out that being a Scorpio, I was a water sign. She told me that she could tell I was water because my movements were so feminine and graceful, the very words I would have used to describe her. My heart literally opened up as she shared that she was a Cancer, also a water sign. To have anything in common with such a goddess, lifted me sky high and I was now hooked for life.

I also started asking my fellow dancers what their signs were and found I was surrounded by fire and earth dancers. No wonder I had felt so out of place.

I'll always be grateful to Jeena for the insight she gave me, for comparing me with herself and for giving me the inspiration to keep dancing. I saw her a few more times and learned more from her, but then she disappeared and I have no idea where she is or if she is still dancing. I do know she is still with me in spirit.

My next teacher, and life-long mentor, was Halima. Halima is a walking encyclopedia of belly dancing. She is one of the smartest people I know and one of the best dancers I have ever met. But, beyond her brains and skill as a dancer, she also possesses a rare wisdom and is a very nurturing friend.

Saheena and I brought Halima to Coos Bay for several workshops. She is the one who taught me about good posture, and how to position my arms. I learned so much from her, not only how to dance, but also about the history and culture. Like I said, she is an encyclopedia of belly dance knowledge.

It wasn't long before Saheena and I asked two of our students, Tina and Ann to join us, and we formed our first troupe called, Troupe Shikhat. We named ourselves after the women of the Shikhat tribe whom we perceived as the first women libbers. These women went from

Halima

their mountain villages into the towns and danced on the streets for money, collecting enough for their own dowry and returning to their villages where they then purchased a husband. The money stayed with the woman even after divorce, and unlike most Middle Eastern tribes, the woman could request/demand a divorce.

We had a lot of fun with Tina and Ann. On one trip, we went to Seattle to take a workshop and watch a show. Somehow we ended up with part of the band driving around Seattle. The drummer was Arabic and was driving, talking and showing us drumming techniques all at once, while driving at a high speed. We never forgot that experience as we prayed for our lives flying up and down hills through Seattle. I don't remember where we were going, but I'll always remember that ride.

We danced together as a troupe for about a year, and were the best of friends doing everything together. Our children played together while we visited. Our husbands played music for us and became friends; then the worst happened. First Saheena and her husband got divorced, than my husband and Ann had an affair. It was devastating. To make a very long and traumatic story short, Saheena moved away, I moved out, and Ann moved in with my husband. Tina was too traumatized to deal with it all, and the troupe was dissolved. It was like my own personal soap opera. My friends were gone, and I was alone again!

But, not for long! I continued to teach on my own, and I made more friends in the dance. For instance, there was my friend, Joan, a teacher at our local college and her husband, Joe who ended up encouraging me to go back to college. (I did, and I got a degree in human services.)

Over the years, I have traveled to workshops to learn more, and on my travels I've met more friends, and my circle widened.

My friendship with Halima has spanned over 30 years, and she has been there for me through thick and thin. She has been a constant anchor in the storms of my life, helping me cope with three (yes, three) divorces always ready to lend loving support and advice. Her wisdom is a rare commodity in this world, and I can turn to her during any life crisis and find solace and helpful advice.

At my surprise 50th birthday party, Ameena who was a student in my very first belly dance class came and danced for me giving me a blown up photo of myself dancing 25 years before. She and I have been friends from the beginning, and she went on from that first class to out-dance her teacher (me) and become a well-known professional in our field. We have lots of shared dance memories and continue to create new ones.

My current troupe, Mystical Oasis Dance Company has brought me an amazing community of women. Jasel and Masahti are our oldest members. Jasel is my right hand and sometimes my left. She fills the room with joy, is quite a presence and doesn't have a clue how wonderful she is. Watching her dance is an instant anti-depressant. Mashati is a Goddess incarnate, six feet of love and acceptance. As she dances, her graceful stage presence fills the room with feminine essence. Shaheena is another beautiful dancer and Goddess whose nurturing presence in my life has touched me to the core. Azuul Khayal came to dance class and became a troupe member and daughter of my heart, moving in with me until she went off to the university.

Over the years I have made more friends in the dance then I could ever write about, mostly women, but there are also men.

Most belly dance musicians are men, and one of my first men friends in the dance was Alan Bachman. Halima sponsored his band, 'Desert Wind' in their very first performance and invited me to dance. It was at a place called 'Pa's Cellar' in Portland, Oregon and was situated under 'Ma's Kitchen.' We had great fun, and I still tease Alan about the fact that every fast song he played sounded like the popular Arabic song called, 'Linda, Linda.'

Alan and I have been friends for over 30 years. He is Jewish and is the assistant district attorney for the state of Utah, and his best friend is an Arabic man named Raj, the main drummer in Desert Wind. Needless to say, Alan is diverse and very interesting to have as a friend. He and Raj are living examples that peace can exist between Arabs and Jews and they take every opportunity possible to promote that peace with their music.

My community of dancers extends around the world. I have staff writers and subscribers to my magazine, 'Jareeda' whom I've only met via the internet, but to me they are friends. Sometimes I get to meet them in person at different events, and that's always fun.

One day, my staff writer, Morgana, from Massachusetts contacted me. "Did you know there are belly dancers in Antarctica? She asked? "I want to do an article for 'Jareeda' on this, what do you think?" I told her, that yes I did know there were belly dancers in Antarctica and that I knew one of them who was from Oregon. It really is a small world. So Morgana wrote a great article about the belly dancers in Antarctica. We are everywhere!!! It helps that in real life, she is a professional journalist, and her articles are always well-researched and interesting. She's a great asset to the magazine and I was so happy to finally meet her in person.

One of my long-time subscribers is from New Orleans. We had been in touch off and on over the years, and she told me that if I ever got to New Orleans, I was welcome to stay in her guest house. Then, one day she emailed me that she was coming to visit her daughter in Portland, Oregon, and she wondered if we could meet in person. As it turned out, Hurricane Katrina hit just after she arrived in Oregon, and she ended up staying much longer then she had originally planned.

The Double Crown Belly Dance Competition was happening soon, so I contacted the sponsor, and asked her if she would consider allowing my friend to be one of the judges. She had never been to a competition, but I knew with her years of experience, she would be a competent and fair judge. She and her husband attended the event, and it was wonderful to meet them both in person. They helped me with my vending table, helped judge, and for a few hours they had something fun and different to do to take their mind off of the tragedy back home.

Once you are part of the belly dance community, you can move or travel anywhere in the world and have instant friends. It is like being part of a huge extended family. Belly dancers come from all walks of life, from all backgrounds, religions and cultures, but we all have the dance in common. The dance is a common language that crosses borders and overcomes obstacles and limitations between races and cultures. In a way, we are messengers of peace and acceptance.

When I meet a belly dancer from another country, we may not be able to speak each other's languages of words, but we do speak dance, music, costuming and a shared joy. There is nothing like the feeling of being connected to women around the world.

Our dance transcends time and space. Our sisterhood transcends time and space. The movements that I do when I dance are ancient movements that my sisters did thousands of years ago, movements my sisters thousands of years into the future will be doing. These movements are also being done by women all over the planet in Afghanistan, Japan, Australia, China, Russia, Germany, Argentina, Iran and Iraq. You name the country and there's probably a belly dancer there.

I feel a sense of achievement and gratitude when I think how a tiny part of me will live forever through the dance. It is an amazing thing to be a part of such a continuum of community that knows no barriers.

One of the best things I have done is to sponsor a belly dance retreat for women only. For one weekend a year, we create our own special community. My first camp was at a Girl Scout campground, a very rustic place. It had running water, but the water was contaminated with Giardia making it a health hazard. It did have flushing toilets, showers and a small kitchen. There were three-walled cabins, and a couple of us camped in tents. My son was a nursing infant, and didn't feel well. He screamed the entire night. Between him and the dive bombing bats, people had little rest.

That first retreat had seven instructors and seven students. We had fun despite the contaminated water, unhappy baby and assorted forest creatures. In fact, we bonded so closely that many of us have maintained friendships over the years until the present.

Now my retreat has been going on for 24 years and I'm looking forward to my 25th anniversary. Each year we have ten or more teachers and 80-100 dancers in attendance. We learn from each other and we have three nights of performing for each other. Each year is magical, mystical and healing.

There is nothing like an all woman event. It's not that we don't love men; it's just a different energy when it's all women. One weekend, Halima wore her nightie the whole weekend; she never got dressed. She oversaw the workshops from the porch of the kiosk and was dubbed, the "Porch Goddess." If men had been in attendance, she would have gotten dressed; you know it, and it just wouldn't have been the same.

Then there was the year the twin towers went down. That happened on September 11, 2001. My retreat was scheduled to start on Sept 14, 2001. The country was in shock and mourning. I received phone calls and emails from dancers around the country. "Should we cancel our event?" "We are canceling our belly dance show because we are afraid people will harass us." "Are you going to cancel your retreat?"

Dancers everywhere were afraid to be doing a dance of the Middle East when we had just been attacked by people from the Middle East. My response was, "DO NOT LET THEM WIN!"

For most of us, belly dancing is more than a dance, more than exercise or performing. It has become a lifestyle and our connection to others whether it is other dancers, our audiences or just people in the towns where we live. We take pride in what we do, and as I stated earlier, it is a dance that crosses borders.

While some dancers put their dancing on hold for awhile after 911, I felt that it was important to keep on dancing. It was important to educate people and show them a beautiful aspect of the Middle East. I don't know of one dancer who experienced negativity as a result of 911. I don't think American people equated belly dancing with terrorists.

For me, it gave an opportunity to educate the public. It opened a new door of awareness for some. I explained that the terrorists were fanatics, not a true representation of the Muslim people. In Christianity, there are also fanatics and different sects. For instance, there is the sect in the south who handles rattlesnakes during church services. Are rattlesnake handlers the only representation of Christianity? When I explained this to people, it helped them to understand, and it also helped them let go of their fears. What a scary thing it is to believe that all Muslims are terrorists!

The dance is a bridge between our cultures, a bridge that I use to communicate with as well as educate, and I believe that the more we dance, the more understanding and tolerance we will have in our world.

So, back to my retreat in 2001... I did have misgivings about it. I had no idea if people would show up or how the weekend would go. I just knew that I wasn't going to let terrorists stop me from doing anything.

That weekend all of the registrants except two showed up. One of them had emergency surgery and the other's daughter went into premature labor. Everyone else was there. I did have six teachers cancel due to airport shut downs and one worked for the Red Cross and couldn't get away. As people were checking in, I asked six of them to teach a workshop, and all said yes, no problem.

It was my most intense retreat ever. Each retreat we do a campfire circle and morning visualization. That year, I flew by the seat of my pants and it ended up being a beautiful experience. After the campfire circle, we all held hands, over eighty women in a circle, and I led us in my version of prayer. I asked that as a group we all focus on sending loving light to the victims of the bombing, and to their families and friends. Then I asked that we send loving light to the families of the terrorists. I said a lot more just letting Spirit speak through me and not knowing what people would think or feel, but hoping they would all understand my intent and join me in sending light.

The next morning, I led a visualization, not about the dance as I usually do, but about healing and sending healing to the sights of the bombings. We did similar things a couple of more times over the weekend, and it helped all of us.

Yes, we did dance that weekend, and we did laugh and share joy as well as sadness. One dancer told me she was recently from New York and had eaten her lunch every day in the plaza below the twin towers. She said she had felt guilty about coming to the retreat and doing something fun after such a horrible tragedy, and but mostly she had felt terribly helpless. She told me that she was so glad she had come because she no longer felt guilty and helpless and knew she was in the right place at the right time and she thanked me. Other dancers also expressed similar sentiments of wanting to help but not knowing how. They said that the circles where we sent prayers helped them feel like they were doing something, that they were helping in an energetic way by sending healing. As a group, it was a very powerful experience, and we could all feel the energy and our common intent to help with healing. It was truly amazing, empowering and powerful.

I no longer feel isolated and alone in the world. I have a community of friends around the world, and we are truly like an extended family. Every event I attend is like a family reunion. I always spend the first part of the event hugging and catching up on news.

7 FAMILY

The dance has given me many things, but uppermost is an extended family. My parents disowned me several years ago. It was like the final abuse. Part of me mourned and part of me felt free after a life-time of seeking their love and approval. I really don't know for sure why I was disowned, but I haven't heard from my parents, sisters, aunts, uncles or cousins in over 18 years. My family is my kids and grandkids, and my chosen family members, sisters and brothers I've met through the dance.

Dancing with my daughter was a highlight of my life. We moved together in perfect synchronicity, and it always felt like we had a mind link and were extensions of each other. I loved dancing with Avena, who chose the name, Sativa for a dance name. I've danced with many women over the years, but nothing compares to dancing with my girl.

As an adult, she became quite the professional in her career and also my computer guru and the mother to my beautiful grandchildren. What a beautiful blessing she is, and I cherish her.

I had hoped that my son, Logan, would become a drummer so that someday we could drum and dance together, but he has his own path. He's a musician, alright, but heavy metal guitar doesn't go too well with belly dance. I love that he is as passionate about his music as I am about my dance.

My favorite Logan story was when he was nine years old. One day he asked me, "Mom? How come you're so weird?" I asked him if it was because I was a belly dancer, and he said yes. I had danced his whole life, had even danced with him in my belly, and one day he realized that no one else's mom belly danced so his mom must be weird.

I asked him if he'd like it better if I stopped dancing, and he said, "Oh no, mom. You love it too much!" What a guy!

So, I explained that weird just meant different and that it was a good thing to be different, and later I overheard him advising a friend about how it was cool to be weird. Love, love, love, my boy.

Naomi, aka Azuul Khayal, isn't a biological daughter, but daughter of my heart. My heart adopted her when she was 16 and showed up in my dance class; she's been a member of our family ever since. She is also such a joy to dance with, and I love watching her perform. When I met her, she was home-schooled and had never been inside of a traditional classroom, but it didn't stop her from going to a university and even a year of schooling in Japan. Pretty amazing, I'd say.

As for dance family members, some I only see once a year, some every few years, and then there was the time I found out that one of my belly dance friends really was blood family!

In 2005, I was asked to teach a seminar at the Tribal Dreams Festival in Lincoln, Nebraska. I had never been to the Midwest, and I absolutely loved it there. I didn't think I would know anyone there, but I was up for the adventure of spending four days in a place I'd never been with people I'd never met. It turned into another magical time in my life.

I left Nebraska feeling like I had made new friends, friends that I would always carry in my heart. I was housed with a belly dancer who was also a minister, so we had a lot in common and a lot to talk about. It was like we'd known each other forever. The sponsors were wonderful women who attract the most wonderful people into their lives.

The absolute highlight of my weekend was seeing a friend I hadn't seen in a few years. Her name is Kathe Alkoudsi and we had met at a belly dance event a few years before and instantly hit it off. We rarely saw each other, but when we did, we had brief but good visits together. Well, this weekend, we had a lot of time to visit, since our vending tables were next to each other. I was telling her about my life, and mentioned being raised on an Apache reservation in Arizona. She asked, "Which reservation??"

I was surprised because no one had ever asked that before; most people don't know there are different reservations of Apachse. I told her it was the San Carlos Tribe. Then she told me she had an aunt who had a trading post in Peridot, Arizona. I instantly broke out in goose bumps over my entire body, and could hardly speak. No one I had ever met knew there was such a place as Peridot.

"What was your aunt's name," I asked, barely able to speak.

"Her name was Joyce Osborne."

I was overwhelmed with emotion, and with tears in my eyes, I said, "That was my grandmother."

So we discovered that we were actually related. She was my mother's first. We were both totally elated, and we announced to anyone who came into the room after that, "She's my cousin!" "Mezdulene's my cousin!" she'd exclaim or "Kathe's my cousin," I'd announce. Everyone joined us in our joy, congratulating us, and listening to our story over and over again.

Kathe told me lots about my family that I never knew since my family wasn't close, proven by the fact we didn't know each other existed. For me it was very emotional because I had been disowned by my family, and here was a family member happy to be related to me. I couldn't wait to call my daughter and tell her, and she was happy for me. She said she was so glad I had finally met a 'nice' relative!

My second husband was the brother-in-law of Saheena, my first dance partner. I first met Jack when he was married to her sister, and I thought he was very handsome, and I also thought they didn't seem to match very well. It wasn't long before he and his wife were divorced, and he lived with Saheena until he could find his own place. I got to know him a bit when I visited Saheena and he would be there, lonely and downcast.

It wasn't long before he found his own place, and soon after that, Saheena was divorced and her husband moved in with him. It became the bachelor pad.

By then, I considered Jack a friend. When Saheena and I put on our first production, she asked him to be one of the Eunuchs who were to carry us to the stage in our litter. That turned into a comedy all its own, a memory that Jack and I will always share. Our Eunuchs were unevenly matched, short on one side and tall on the other. Saheena and I had lit candles in our hands, and we were tossed from side to side as they carried us down the aisle with no way to grab hold and hang on. It took all of our resolve to keep from laughing in hysteria while making our dramatic entrance once they sat us on the stage.

When my first marriage ended with lots of soap opera-like drama, Jack was there for me as a friend and shoulder to cry on. All of my other friends were part of the drama and unavailable, so I was left alone except for him. He asked my daughter and I to have Thanksgiving at the bachelor pad, and as it turned out he asked some street people also, and it was an interesting holiday to say the least. There was the hugely obese vegetarian woman who screamed when she caught her two year old grabbing hands full of turkey and scarfing it down as fast as he could. I was wondering how a vegetarian could be so obese but soon found out when she cut the huge chocolate cake exactly in half and put one half on her plate eating it entirely by herself.

The first time Jack asked me out, he asked if he could take me and my daughter out to eat. The fact that he included Avena meant a lot to me. We ended up moving in together, and eventually marrying, but our marriage didn't last. Jack had met me through the dance, but as it turns out, he didn't like me dancing. Sometimes he'd accuse me of dancing for sailors, which would make me laugh, but it was obvious he was worried I'd find someone else. He wanted me to quit dancing, and that was something I couldn't do. I felt it was like asking me to cut out my guts, and that I would never ask him to quit something he loved. That just wasn't what love was about. Where was the trust?

We tried to work things out, tried counseling together, but it just wasn't meant to be. We did create a great kid together, and we parted amicably. Jack is still family, the father of my son and he will always be a friend.

I spent four years alone, a single mom with a teenager and toddler. They were years of personal growth and healing, and years of closeness with the sisters of my heart. My friends, whom I had met through the dance, and I formed a woman's group, and we met each month. Each month our meetings took us to a new place, and each month was healing. We were there for each other no matter what. Never have I felt so nurtured, and I will always consider these women my sisters. Even though I moved away, I hold them in my heart and I visit them when I can.

And, speaking of family, one of my oldest friends, Tiana, became my mother-in-law. I met her over 30 years ago at a belly dance event and we became very close. I lived on the Oregon coast, and she lived 80 miles inland and when I needed an escape, I would head for her house. When she needed an escape, she'd head for mine. Our daughters were only a year apart, and when we visited each other, our girls would have all night marathons of talk and laughter. When my son was born, he was a part of Tiana's Gypsy belly dance show at only three months of age.

One day, Tiana called me and told me that she and her family were at the coast fishing and she asked me to come join them. She told me her son was with them, and she thought we would really hit it off. My first thought was why would I be interested in her son? I'm not a cradle robber. I was thinking our daughters were the same age, forgetting that she had told me her son was almost grown when she had her daughter. I looked forward to visiting her, so I went and met them at the dock. She introduced me to her son, Tim. He had a cap and sunglasses on and he nodded, grunted a greeting then quickly turned back to fishing.

After the dock, we headed for the beach. Tiana was cavorting with her grandkids, and I had my son and we were having fun in the waves. Tim was lounging on the beach, and I went to encourage him to join us. He no longer had on his sunglasses, and when I looked into his eyes, I was a goner. He was gorgeous with a soul as deep as the sea, and I fell in and became completely submerged.

To make a long love story short, we were married after only two months of knowing each other, and again belly dancers became real family. My mother-in-law, Tiana was a belly dancer. My sister-in-law, Alexa was a belly dancer, and my two nieces, Suzie and Amy, also belly dancers. We were one big belly dancing family.

After my second divorce, I had done a lot of thinking and soul-searching. I didn't ever want to repeat my mistakes and at first I couldn't figure out what my two husbands had in common except for me. My first husband was tall, dark and handsome with piercing blue eyes. He was a know-it-all and a show off, but also brilliant and fascinating. My second husband was shorter, light and handsome. His personality was totally opposite, quiet, modest and fun when things were good. I finally figured out the one thing they had in common. Both had totally dependent mothers who never worked outside the home.

Both of these men were attracted to my independence. I was the total opposite of their mothers, but in reality, after time passed, what they really wanted was someone just like their mother. Both ended up feeling threatened by my independence, and both criticized me after we were married for not being more like their mothers.

So, my solution was to decide if I ever had another man in my life, his mom would be independent like me. Well, this time, my husband was raised with belly dancing, so my dancing was no problem. Tiana wasn't as independent as I am when it comes to traveling or other things, but she has a very strong and independent spirit. And, she is definitely the family matriarch, the one people turn to in times of need whether they need advice or need nursing. She is the strength of the family, the glue that holds it together.

Unfortunately, my marriage to her son also failed. He chose another path, one that didn't include me.

I told people it felt like Spirit just picked up my life and all its components, shook it all around, spilled it back out on the ground, and I had to pick up the pieces and put it back together again.

The loss of my husband, and his family was a great loss. I grieved deeply. I also lost my income, home and car, even more challenges to deal with.

Through it all, my children and the sisters of my heart supported me. They loved me and they lifted me up when I was down. I have never felt so loved and supported, and I have never felt so blessed. There were times when I just wanted to leave the area as if leaving would somehow be leaving the pain, but their support kept me strong.

Now, on the other side of grief, I magically have my house back, and I feel strong and whole. Most of all, I feel freedom for the very first time in my life. I am free to be me. I know that sounds trite, but there is no other way to word it. For the first time I can do whatever I want, whenever I want and for as long as I want without censure. It's absolutely wonderful.

As I write this, my life is better than it's ever been before. It's a life filled with dance, love and joy. Who could ask for more?

8 MUSIC

Belly dance music is different than what most Americans are used to hearing, but at the same time, it's compelling and addicting.

I once had an angry husband confront me. He said that his wife, my student, used to cook dinner every night, but now all she did was practice dancing and warm up TV dinners in the microwave. She used to make quilts, but now all she did was bead on her damn costumes. But the worst thing of all is that she used to listen to country western music, and now their house was filled with that Arabic crap all hours of the day!

The funny part of this true story is that it was his idea she take lessons thinking it would be sexy to have his wife belly dance for him, and now he was accusing me of creating a monster.

I reminded him that it was his idea for her to take lessons, but he continued to fume and act as if I was some sort of succubus who was using my wiles to cast a spell on his wife. I felt like he got what he deserved!

At first, some of the music was hard for me to listen to also. The mizmar is a reed instrument, ancient and haunting, but it can also reach a pitch that is uncomfortable for my ears.

I'm not a musician, so I can't tell you much about how Middle Eastern music differs from Western music, but it has been explained to me by musicians, something about quarter tones and half tones. All I understood is that it is different and more complicated in some ways then our contemporary music.

What I do know for sure is that the music touches me deeply and calls me to respond. It makes me happy, and it makes me want to dance.

The first music I heard was from the album, 'Oriental Bouquet' by Harry Saroyan. My teacher used music from that album when she did the demo dance at my first class, and I was captivated. It was the most exotic and intoxicating music I had ever heard, and my teacher's performance to it was the most riveting and captivating thing I had ever seen.

Combine the audio with the visual, and I was in bliss. I felt my heart expand, and a feeling came over me; it was as if, for the first time in my life I felt I belonged. I had never seen belly dancing or heard Middle Eastern music before, but it brought me comfort, and felt so familiar.

For the first few years I danced, there really wasn't much music available. I bought every album I could get my hands on. Some were great; some were awful, but each had something to offer, either a call to dance or the lesson. George Abdo and Eddie the Sheik were the top names in music, both from the east coast. I bought every album they put out and danced my heart out to their music.

My first live music experience was with Brothers of Baladi. At the time, they were a duet consisting of Michael Beach, the drummer and Joseph Pucey who played just about everything else, from oud to mizmar, and he sang. Their music was great and very inspiring. You could say, I cut my teeth on live music with them. As I look back, I can see how fortunate I was to have live music so early in my dance career. They played for us whenever they passed through town; every time I was asked to dance, and every time it was a blast!

The Brothers of Baladi are still going strong all these years later, although Joseph has since passed away, a great sadness for our dance community. They have several CDs on the market, each one unique.

One of my dance highlights was performing with my partner, Saheena, in Seattle to live music with George Abdo. For some of the dancers, his band played alone so I didn't expect him to sing for us, and when he did, I almost swooned. His voice was incredible. Forget Frank Sinatra; give me George Abdo any day! The whole time we were dancing, it was like I was in a dream, a surreal experience. When I turned my back to the audience, there he was singing and it was amazing! I was on the stage with the most popular Middle Eastern singer of my generation!

It was years before I topped that experience.

Early in my career, my dance mates and I went to a show in Seattle featuring music by the band 'Sirocco' from Northern California. We arrived early and had nowhere else to go, so we sat in our car waiting for the doors to open. Parked next to us was a van with music equipment and musicians; they were also early. We ended up talking to them and having a great time. Armando was a cuddly teddy bear, and Sulieman, a friendly lecher who kissed my bare foot. We had a great time chatting and hanging out, but the real treat was their music that night in the show. It was folksy and upbeat but also had some moving slow pieces. We had a blast! To this day, they are on the top of my music list.

Another group I met early on is 'Desert Wind' with members Alan Bachman playing the keyboard and drummer, Bob Dexter. I mentioned earlier that I danced with them at Pa's Cellar under Ma's Kitchen in Portland, Oregon, an interesting venue for my first live music experience, but one Alan and I will always remember. It's a memory we both cherish, and we sometimes remind ourselves of our humble beginnings and the beginning of our friendship.

My other memory, besides the one where all the fast music sounded similar, was stepping on a glass bead during my performance and bleeding all over the dance floor. The beads on our costumes are made from glass, and after that experience I became quite the advocate for sweeping the stage after beaded fringe breaks and spills beads on the floor.

Several years ago, Desert Wind put out some albums with Goddess music and Middle Eastern rhythms called, Gaia, Kali Ma and Return to the Goddess. This combination made perfect sense to me, and I absolutely loved this music. To this day, I use it constantly in class and for performance.

I believe that our dance form evolved from the time of Goddess worship, thousands of years ago before written history, a time when woman was revered for her child-bearing ability and her ability to nourish life by producing food for the newborn. Now, remember, this was before men knew they had a part in this and society was matriarchal.

Ancestry was traced through the mother because after all, everyone knew who the mother was. This just seems like common sense even in our current day and age.

So, belly dance music honoring the Goddess was perfect and it called me to dance to it and to create a dance form called Goddess Dancing. I developed this form of dance for every woman, not just for belly dancers. Any woman can do this dance even those who have no dance training at all.

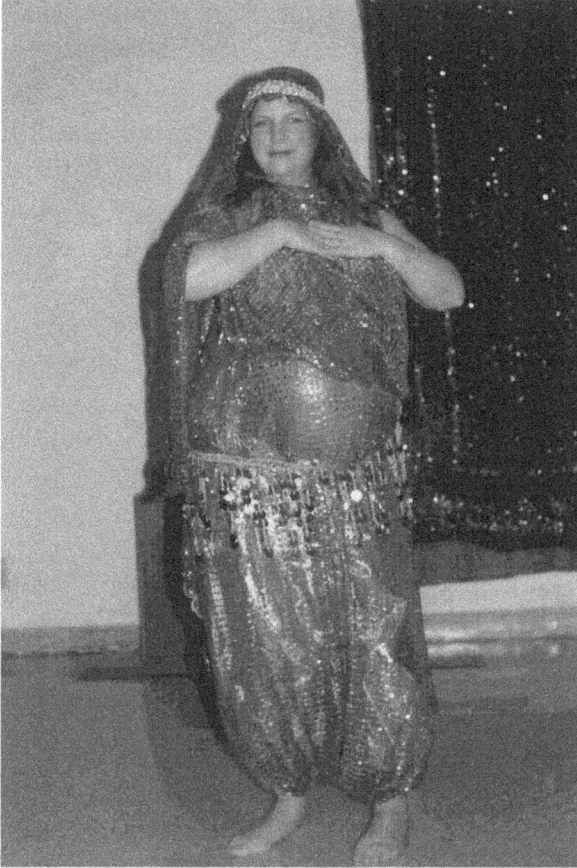

Doing the dance of the Mother Goddess at full term.

I have been challenged a few times because I call it Goddess dancing, and that's 'not Christian,' however, it has nothing to do with Goddess worship. I gave this some deep thought. I'm not a Goddess worshiper, but this dance is about 'the Goddess.' This dance honors the Goddess within each woman. We all have Goddess aspects, and belly dance helps put us in touch with that part of ourselves and helps us empower and strengthen those divine feminine aspects.

Each dance expresses our femininity, and it is awesome to watch a roomful of women, some mothers, some barren, some choosing not to bear children, all expressing the womanly essence of birthing and nurturing.

One of the dances I include was given to me many years ago by a friend, and I believe it originated with Jamilla Salimpour in San Francisco. It is a dance of the Mother Goddess where a poem is recited along with the music, and a dancer dances the words of the poem. This dance is powerful, and although I use it in my workshops, I don't allow women to perform it without a warning. If you are fertile at all, and you don't want to get pregnant, don't perform this dance. I've had two dancers on birth control become pregnant immediately after doing this dance in performance.

My preference is pregnant women performing this dance. I first performed it when I was nine months pregnant with my son, and it was amazing. In 2004, my sister-in-law did the dance while I recited the poem to the live music of Desert Wind and Americanistan. It was so potent; the audience was in total awe, and I became overpowered by emotion. With her huge belly painted with mother earth, and her beautiful, feminine energy filling the space, there is no way to put into words the intensity of feeling in that room.

One of my greatest music highlights came when I traveled to Egypt. Egyptian music has a flavor all its own, and until traveling to Egypt, I wasn't a fan. I'm still not too thrilled with a lot of the recorded Egyptian music, however it was an entirely different experience to hear it live. Much of the music from Egypt is orchestrated and sounds too modern for my taste, but dancing to it live was a rapturous experience. In America, I had experienced a five member band at the most, but in Egypt, the orchestras had more finger cymbal players then that. The bands ranged from a couple of guys with a drum and a mizmar to a full orchestra complete with violins. Both were quite the experience, one that I can never really adequately describe.

Dancing in Egypt was definitely a career highlight; the music filled me with such an intense feeling of being connected, grounded and accepted. It was an all time natural high; I will always treasure and never forget.

More recently, Americanistan came on the scene. The leaders of the band are Dunyah al Hanna and Omar, or Denise and Wayne Gilbertson. While their band members have come and gone over the years, Janet

Naylor has been one constant. I have been honored to watch them evolve from the beginning into my all time favorite band to dance with. They even named a song after me called, "Queen Mez." I was deeply touched and thrilled to death. Like Desert Wind, they play both Arabic and Hebrew music, but they have an entirely different flavor of sound, more earthy and at the same time ethereal.

While I love the sound of their music, I love even more how I feel when I dance to their music. Together, we create a synergy of healing energy. When I dance with Americanistan, I can actually feel pure love flowing through me at an intense rate and flowing out to the audience touching them with healing and filling me with an empowering feeling of bliss.

Once, I even had an on stage, personal healing take place. For a few weeks I had been experiencing vertigo, headaches and blurred vision. I couldn't figure out what was wrong, and I was too busy and anti-doctor to really look into the problem. I knew these were symptoms of high blood pressure, but I have always had low blood pressure, so didn't believe it could be high blood pressure.

The day before my annual belly dance festival and show featuring Americanistan, I finally went to the fire station and asked a paramedic to take my blood pressure just to rule it out. Was I ever surprised when he told me it wasn't just a tad elevated, but very elevated! Well, the mystery of my symptoms was solved, but I didn't have time to deal with it because my festival and show were the very next day. I would deal with it later.

The whole day of my festival I functioned in a fog. My vision was blurred, and the roomful of noise seemed to reverberate in my skull. It took every ounce of my stamina to make it through the day.

I had vertigo, blurred vision and no balance, but nothing short of being unconscious was going to keep me from dancing that night with Americanistan. Shortly after coming on stage, I began to feel the love and healing energy start to flow through me. About half way through my dance something amazing occurred. My vision suddenly cleared and the buzzing in my head stopped. I felt a euphoric sense of well-being flow through my body and I knew I was healed. I was so amazed! I danced up to Dunyah and said, "I just had a healing," and then danced away as she gave me a sweet smile.

The next day I returned to the fire station, and again had my blood pressure taken. This time it was back to my normal relaxed pressure. I had it taken several more times in the next few weeks and it was always normal. I'm not sure why I had high blood pressure, but I do know that I was healed that night, and in the years since have never had those symptoms again.

I always knew that I felt something special when I danced with Americanistan, but I didn't know they shared my feelings until one night Wayne told me that when I dance, I take them to the temple. He said they loved playing for me because they could just let go and allow the music to flow out and let whatever happened, happen. It is definitely a spiritual experience for all of us, and I feel very blessed to say the least to have them in my life.

Another musical high for me occurred at my retreat a few years ago. Dunyah came and taught a class of chanting where she led us in several chants while some of us drummed. That night, we had live music dubbed the AGAS (Ahh Gaahs) by Dunyah or All Girl All Stars. When it was my turn to dance, I didn't really have a request. Dunyah suggested chanting for me while I danced, and that's what happened.

Again, words fail me, but I will try to give you a sense of what I experienced. 80 women chanting for me while I danced was the most beautiful music I have ever heard. Angels? Goddesses? Nymphs? Priestesses? All of the above were there for me as the music entered me and flowed through me into movements. I reached out to all of them as the love flowed through me to them and their love flowed back to me in huge waves of emotion. Together, we transcended time and space traveling to a place of bliss so intense that I can't imagine anything more remarkable. When the song ended, I literally sobbed with emotion, and I have not been the same since then. That night, I touched something eternal, something sacred and powerful. I hold it in my heart and in my mind. It is always there for me, and I am blessed.

I know many dancers who will only dance to CDs. Some of them only dance with choreography and some improvise but want to know exactly what is coming next in the music. In some ways, I'm a control freak myself, so I can relate to the fact that they want to maintain control over their dance. Live music takes that control away.

However, I feel they are missing out on so much, missing out on what the essence of the dance really is, the expression of music through dance in the moment. It's an ancient art form from a time long before recorded music existed, and part of its appeal for me is the freedom this expression allows.

For the longest time, I couldn't understand why anyone would choose a CD over live music until recently. A good friend of mine explained it this way: "Improvisation is not where my art lies. My art is in choreography. When I choreograph, I listen to the song for a few weeks before I ever start choreographing it. I learn every nuance of the song, I begin to get visions of the dance, and I literally SEE it in my mind's eye. I visit with this song literally hundreds of times, and I dance with it until the song tells me what it wants. I paint a picture with movement of what I believe the music tell me it wants me to do."

For me, choreography is limiting to my soul, and improvisation is my art. I can dance to the same piece of music repeatedly and paint a different picture each time depending on my mood, the energy of the audience, what's going on in the world and a hundred other details. I allow the music to move through me and my body expresses what it's telling me like a story, and each time I dance to a piece, it's like another aspect of the story or another color on the palette. To me, choreography is like painting by numbers using the same colors each time in the same place instead of being free to just paint what I feel.

And, this is one reason our dance is such an incredible art form. It allows each dancer to create in the way that feels right to them. It's not an exact discipline; it's truly art.

9 CLEOPATRA, EMISSARY OF LOVE

One stormy night, I headed to a dance gig up the coast. It was a private party put on by Roxanna, a belly dance friend, for her husband's co-workers and friends. It was an elaborate affair complete with catering and dancers, and attended by the upper echelon of the community.

After the party was over and most people had left, Roxanna brought out her snake, Cleopatra. It was love at first sight. She handed me Cleo and I was fascinated by her beauty and completely charmed by her character. As we continued to visit, Cleo curled up right on top of my heart, and just quietly hung out.

As it turns out, Roxanna wanted to sell Cleo and I went home with a new friend. She was a ball python and had beautiful markings. She moved slowly and deliberately unless it came to food time and then she moved quicker than the eye could follow.

I loved her, and she loved me; she became my symbol of unconditional love. Unlike other animals that purr and rub on your leg or yip and jump up and down with excitement when you enter the room, Cleo let me know energetically that she completely and unconditionally loved me.

As I got to know her better, I understood how in tune she was with energy, and how much she and I were alike when it came to what kind of energy we liked or didn't like. For instance, if she didn't like someone and they were holding her, she would keep crawling away. In order to keep holding her, they would have to keep 'reeling' her in or pulling her back as she kept trying to crawl away. If she liked someone, she was content to let them hold her and would most likely crawl up their sleeve or down their shirt wanting to get close and snuggly.

Some belly dancers dance with snakes, so I decided I would give it a try. I danced with Cleo several times, and found that it was a like dancing with a small child; it didn't really matter what I did, all eyes were on the kid or the snake. Ha ha!

Dancing with Cleopatra.

I would bring her out onto the stage in a basket balanced on my head, then put the basket down front and center. I'd dance a bit and then do some hand movements over the top of the basket, then open the lid and reach in to get her out. My favorite times were when she would push the lid up herself and poke her head out.

It turns out Cleo loved dancing as much as I did. She loved the music, and wasn't afraid of the room full of energy. And, of course, she trusted me not to drop her. One of the things I always did was dance with her for awhile and then set her on my head. The middle of her body would be on top and she would hang down and hold onto my head and curl her head and tail around wherever. I once had someone come in late, missing the first part of my dance and say, "What a beautiful headpiece you were wearing. Where did you get it?"

"Oh that was my snake." She couldn't comprehend what the heck I was saying, and of course I started laughing at the puzzled/horrified look on her face.

Because there are so many people afraid of snakes, I always made sure it was announced that I was dancing with a snake so that people could move back if they were fearful. I didn't want to scare anyone or cause a heart attack.

One time, the husband of a dancer who was always very supportive of the dance was in the front row. He was one of those tough, manly men, and he was also inebriated and didn't listen to the announcement. When I lifted Cleo out of the basket, he screamed like a little girl and leapt backwards over two rows of seating then ran screaming from the room. It was one of the most amazing things I've ever seen and it took everything in my power to maintain my composure and regain my audience after they burst into laughter.

Another time I had seventeen dancers staying at my home after a show and I heard quite a ruckus in the living room which was right next to my bedroom. Apparently someone decided to turn the light off inside what they thought was just a glass display shelf but was actually Cleo's decorated cage where she was hiding under the rug. As the dancer reached in, Halima told her she couldn't turn the light off because the snake would get cold. Squealing and commotion commenced keeping my poor husband awake and cranky.

Several times, I took Cleo into schools and gave talks about snakes and let the children pet her. Every time, I'd ask who was afraid of snakes, and over half of the kids would raise their hand. Then I'd invite them to pet her, and they would come forward tentatively and then exclaim when they felt how smooth and soft she was. By the time I was done, only one or two didn't touch her.

I also had two close friends who were terrified of snakes and couldn't be in the same room with one even if it was in a cage. They both warmed up to Cleo, one of them even able to touch her. She was an amazing emissary and helped many people get over their fears.

This is perhaps my best Cleo story. My daughter wanted to compete in a belly dance contest when she was nine years old. I can't remember why we took Cleo; one of us planned to dance with her. What I do remember very clearly is that we took a lunch break and before leaving for lunch, I tied Cleo in a pillow case and put her in the suitcase trunk of a vendor.

We had a great lunch, but when we got back, Cleo was gone! Somehow she had escaped! The venue was a big gym at a school, and it was filled with people. I went into a panic. Cleo was like my baby, and she was gone. Where could she possibly be? Also, people are afraid of snakes. I couldn't just make an announcement.

"Excuse me everyone. My python has escaped; can you help me look for her?" Can you imagine the panic that would cause?

So, I quietly went around the room and alerted people, and then I stood and just tried to 'tune in' to Cleo. I know it sounds weird, but she and I were totally connected. If she was hungry, she'd send me a dream. So I walked slowly around the room and 'felt' for her. Inside the vendor's booth where I had left her, I felt her very strongly, but we dug through everything and couldn't find her anywhere. I stood there about to cry, and then felt her again and looked down. She had crawled into the baseboard heater and all I could see was her little head looking up at me.

Well, we had to dismantle the heater to get her free, and that was the last trip Cleo ever took. She was an escape artist which wasn't a problem at home, so home she stayed.

Cleo died a few years ago, and I was heart-broken. I know it sounds strange to be so attached to a snake, but she was very special and touched the hearts of many. I've tried to own other snakes since then, but didn't feel connected to any of them and ended up giving them away.

10 IT'S ALL ABOUT STYLE

When I first started dancing, things were simpler. We danced either cabaret style or folkloric. Now there is cabaret, folkloric, Egyptian, Tribal, Gypsy, Goth and Fusion which can blend any of these with Hip Hop and other forms of dance.

I usually say, it's all belly dancing, and it's all good. I've recently started having some concerns which I'll get into later. First things first....

American Cabaret is the style of dancing that I originally learned, which is now sometimes referred to as 'old style.' The costuming was fairly simple. We wore bras and belts over harem pants and skirts, and we used zills and veils. Our stomachs were bare and the bras and belts were covered with either coins or beads.

We learned steps from many countries in the Middle East. The steps were named things like Arabic basic, Egyptian spin, Syrian sidestep and Moroccan toe pound. We also learned what was called 'veilwork' and 'floorwork.'

We learned that the dance had five parts, and that each part represented an aspect of a woman's life.

The first part of the performance is a fast entrance. The dancer enters with a veil wrapped around her costume; her movements were fast and happy representing her childhood.

The next part is veil dancing and represents puberty and coming into womanhood. The veil is unwrapped leaving the dancer's beautiful costume exposed. The veil movements are executed as the dancer swirls the fabric around creating a beautiful vision. The unveiling is the

74

blossoming of puberty and dancing with the veils is becoming a woman. It can be a very sensual, yet vibrant aspect of performance.

The third part of the routine is usually a drum solo and again, fast. It represents marriage which is the highlight of a woman's life in the Middle East and a huge celebration filled with excitement and anticipation. This part of the dance includes a lot of hip movements, such as shimmies, sometimes containing tension, sometimes loose, but always fast.

Next comes floor dancing. This represents childbirth, another huge milestone in a woman's life. The dancer goes to the floor either with an unexpected drop or slowly and carefully depending on her own style and abilities. She then dances on her knees doing many of the movements done standing up. She also performs movements on her side such as the undulating, 'Cleopatra,' and backbends, belly rolls and body circles. Floor dancing is the most demanding aspect of the dance and takes a lot of strength and training. Sometimes dancers substitute what is called a standing 'taqseem' where movements are done slow and fluid-like.

The last part of the dance routine is again fast, representing the woman celebrating because her children are grown and she gains a sense of more freedom. The dancer usually moves around the stage more and dances with abandonment and joy.

I'm not sure if this is traditional in the Middle East or just an American tradition, but either way, it's nice to celebrate all aspects of a woman's life in dance.

In cabaret style, we always used zills, veils and did floorwork. It was mostly a solo affair. I knew of only two dance troupes the first couple of years I danced. While we all had a similar format, each dancer had her own unique flair, her own unique stage presence and essence.

After a few months of dance classes, three of my friends and I choreographed a dance together. For the first time, I saw myself on video. Ishtar's husband filmed us doing our first dance. He had bought a video camera, the first of its kind available to the general public, a giant thing before batteries that had to be plugged into the wall. As we gathered around watching it, I remember being amazed by two things. First, I was shocked that I was graceful. I had never seen myself in that way in even my wildest imagination. Second, we were all doing the same steps, yet we looked totally different. Each of our bodies expressed each step differently. You could visually see that we were doing the same movements, but you could also see that they looked different on each of us. Although I had big hips, my movements were graceful, more contained and delicate. Ishtar, a very slender woman had large, soft hip movements. Saheena had small, sharp hips while Marissa's hip movements were large and loose. It was fascinating to watch, and to this day I am still mesmerized by a group of women all doing the same dance, yet still each expressing it as an individual. I wish I had a copy of that original video!

As it turns out, the veil aspect of our dance was mostly contributed by Americans. While they use veils in the Middle East, they are more of an entrance prop. The dancer makes her entrance with the veil, quickly swirling around the stage and then dropping it. Here in America, we made the veil an incredible visual art form.

Unless you have seen it, you wouldn't believe how beautiful a three yard piece of fabric can be made to appear. Veils come in various fabrics and sizes. When, I first took lessons, we mostly used long rectangles of chiffon. Chiffon is a see-through and sensual fabric. My teacher only taught five or six different veil movements, but I spent hours playing with my veil and coming up with more and more movements on my own.

I fell totally in love with veil dancing. At first it was my crutch to help me past the shyness. I imagined the audience was watching the flow of my veil, instead of watching me. It was my security blanket. By the time I was done with the veil part of my dance, I was over the initial stage fright and starting to have fun.

As time went on, we began to dance with silk, then circular veils, and then double veils creating more beautiful moves as we went in between the veils using them as a frame for our movements, draping them around us and swirling them like wings. Silk became my favorite fabric because it seems to have a life of its own. To me, veil dancing is the closest thing to flying while still being on the ground.

As an audience member, I love watching veil dancing. It's a visual delight to watch a dancer as she gracefully swirls around the stage using her veil to sculpt different patterns, a true moving art form.

The floor dancing is the most athletic aspect of the dance. It involves back bends and holding yourself up with one hand while lying on your side. To me, it's not fun. When I was younger, floorwork helped me get into the best shape of my life, but it wasn't my favorite part of the dance. It's a vulnerable position to be in, and I always felt self-conscious.

I love watching a dancer do good floorwork, but in my opinion, very few dancers can pull it off well. The floor is where dancers are the most awkward, the least graceful. It takes a lot of strength to look good on the floor and if a dancer isn't strong, she ends up looking like she is struggling to get into position or straining to hold herself up. It also takes proper attitude to do a good job on the floor. It should be feminine and sensual, but some dancers end up looking suggestive. Floorwork is a position where dancers often go more within themselves and don't project as much, which is great, but there needs to be a balance. There is such a thing as building too much tension and making the audience uncomfortable. Putting off sexual and suggestive vibes also makes an audience uncomfortable, and in my opinion crosses the line into territory I don't like seeing belly dancers enter.

American cabaret is still my favorite style of dancing to watch because of its diversity. I especially love the veil, but also love zilling and good floorwork.

When I first started dancing, there was also what we called folkloric style. Dancers did what I called ethnic dances. We learned Turkish line dancing, Greek line dancing and debkes. The dances were always done in groups, and we usually wore Ghawazee coats and Gaza dresses with some sort of head piece, more of a countrified look using plain fabrics instead of fancy. The folkloric was fun, but the movements were less intricate and it wasn't as entertaining to watch from an audience standpoint.

Next on the scene was classical Egyptian dancing which swept through America and the world. This style originates in Egypt, it is less diverse but much more technical. It involves chest and pelvic locks and more precise shimmies. The movements are kept tighter and closer to the body, with less stage coverage. The veil consists of entering, spinning and discarding, as mentioned above, nothing fancy. Some dancers use zills, but most don't. In Egypt, dancers have musicians who play zills for them. Floorwork is out due to the costuming.

Egyptian-style costumes are limiting. Instead of full circular skirts, the skirts are tight and form-fitting. The costumes are covered with incredible beading and sequins,' so going down onto the floor isn't an option. The music is all Egyptian with lots of accents.

I have to admit, that Egyptian-style is my least favorite type of belly dancing to do or to watch. It's just a personal thing with me. When I dance, I like to go with the flow and allow the music to become a part of me, then my movements become an extension of the music, the dance, my personal essence, my mood, the energy of the audience, and all of it becoming part of the experience that we are sharing.

I don't like using choreography, and most Egyptian stylists I know use choreography. The reason I don't like it is because the dance is a creative process for me in every moment. I might wear the same costume, use the same music more than once, but I never dance the same. My dance is always a creative experience which can change each moment.

I once saw a video of an Egyptian dancer doing a choreographed routine. During the video, there were several costume changes. Obviously, she did the same dance at least six times in six different costumes and each time in the same exact way, then the video was edited together to make it look like magical costume changes during one dance. That's when I knew I could never be an Egyptian style dancer. She looked more like a robot than a dancer. She became very famous in the belly dance world, but only after she opened up and allowed her passion to become a more creative expression.

I feel that this style is limited and lacks diversity. While it does emphasize technique, which I appreciate, rarely do Egyptian style dancers use zills, veilwork is very minimal and floorwork is rare. While I can enjoy watching a really good Egyptian dancer, I am easily bored with the lack of diversity and the lack of stage movement, since a dancer often stands in the same position for most of her routine.

Unfortunately, some Egyptian stylists tend to think that they are the only true belly dancers, that Egyptian style is the only 'real' style, and often look down their noses at the other styles. I don't see this as much in other forms of belly dancing and feel this type of attitude hinders rather than helps belly dancers.

When I was in Egypt, I was mesmerized by the dancing. I could have watched a dancer for hours, despite the lack of veil and floor dancing. It was a completely different experience. The true Egyptians dance from the soul. Their movements have an amazing intricacy that goes beyond technique. Every cell of their body exudes passion, and their expression of the music is deep and breathtaking.

For many years, what I saw in America was usually a very poor imitation. There was really no comparison because it was like apples and oranges. Over time, the American Egyptian-style dancers got better and better, and today there are several that do compare, but it's been a long road. The essence of a culture can't be easily imitated, and the dance in Egypt is an extension of their culture.

Fortunately, many Egyptian stylists are now doing veilwork and using zills, incorporating the great technique of Egyptian style with other aspects of belly dance.

While I was in Egypt, I performed a lot and what I found is that the Egyptian dancers wanted to learn from me as much as I wanted to learn from them. They are artists, and art is not stagnant. I have found that the Egyptian stylists, who look down their noses at other forms of belly dance, forget this very important point. They insist that belly dancing is a certain way, (their way) and forget that as with any other art form, it evolves. The way Egyptians dance now is not the same way they danced years ago, and won't be the same as they will dance in the future.

Next on the scene was Tribal style. This style was started in San Francisco, a totally American concept that has now swept the entire planet. Tribal refers not to a tribe in the Middle East or North Africa as many misunderstand it to be. It is a style done in groups, and tribe refers to the group of women who dance together.

At first, many of us were anti-tribal since it was an American concept and *not really* Middle Eastern, but realistically, it's as Middle Eastern as American cabaret. Both styles have the same roots, and American cabaret added veilwork which is an American concept.

FatChanceBellyDance is the original 'tribe,' and they are still going strong. Now there are tribes all over the earth. I once talked to a tribal style dancer from Australia who told me there were over 50 tribes in her province alone. I've even seen Japanese tribal dancers.

While this style of dance has the same roots as cabaret-style, it's also very different. First of all, it's done only in a group. The women dance together and rotate leadership. The dance is improvisational with the dancers so in tune with each other that they can follow the leader, changing steps instantly as the leader cues and changes even though there is no pre-planning. From the audience viewpoint, it looks as if their dance is choreographed, but amazingly it is improvisational. A good tribal troupe dances with synchronicity as well as the most polished choreographed troupe.

This style was also pretty limited at first. Zills were always used, but there was no veil or floorwork done. I remember the first time I saw FatChance how taken I was by their performance. I couldn't wait to see them again. The second time I saw them, I was still pretty impressed, but the third time I remember thinking it looked the same as the last performances. It was very hypnotic to watch, but it was also very repetitive and the dancer's energy stayed more among themselves on stage, with less projection to the audience then other forms of belly dance.

Now veils and props such as swords, fans and baskets are used, and even floorwork is being done in tribal style. There is much more diversity which I think contributed to it becoming a world-wide phenomenon. Tribal dancers have also started to use some choreography.

Dancing in a group with a tribe of women has a universal appeal. I know that many of my own students often aren't interested in performing solos, but over the years, all of them have danced in the group dances. There is something about that sisterhood on stage that makes it safe to dance, safe to express and at the same time, more fun.

At first, tribal dancers all looked pretty much alike. Their costuming consisted of turbans, Kuchi jewelry, choli tops, large gathered skirts and harem pants. It was almost like a uniform. But, we are women, and women create. Before long, flowers were added to turbans. Then, flared and funky pants replaced the harem pants and skirts for some. Hair adornments became very flamboyant and creative with chop sticks, metal thingies, yarn, feathers and even seashells replacing the turban. Tribal costuming is now anything from Middle Eastern to funk and everything in between.

Tribal dancing has evolved just as all art forms evolved. It is now my second favorite form of belly dance. I love it, and with my troupe we go back and forth between cabaret and tribal-style dancing.

Gypsy dancing was next on the scene, and it is what it sounds like.

The dancer wears a gypsy-looking outfit with the big skirt and fringed scarf, with varied head pieces and jewelry. The dancing is done to Gypsy music and is often mostly belly dance moves with a few Gypsy movements and flourishes thrown in.

Historically, Gypsies came out of Egypt and into India and Europe then around the world from there. The most commonly known Gypsies are European. I was fortunate to see a touring Gypsy show which featured Gypsy singing and dancing from around the world, and it was fantastic.

This dance style started a controversy in the belly dance community. Some dancers were offended by the term 'Gypsy' saying it was an insulting name given to this group of people, and they prefer to be called 'Rom.' I printed more than one article in 'Jareeda' about this, one saying that the term Gypsy was synonymous to the word nigger.

My question was if it is such an insult then why do people travel the world singing and dancing and calling their selves, Gypsies? I consulted with Morocco, knowing that she had a Gypsy heritage and she confirmed that yes it was a derogatory term, and that her own father had to deny his heritage in order to find employment. Supposedly the term comes from being gypped by thieves, and the race of people was then called Gypsies. Cher's song, 'Gypsies, Tramps and Thieves' is an example of the 'Gypsy' stereotype.

But, I also heard that the term came from the fact that Gypsies came from Egypt, and was slang for Egyptians. So who knows where this term came from?

For a while I tried to honor the fact that they wanted to be called Rom. But then I was sent an article written by a friend of mine who is half Gypsy. She says that the term Rom comes from Romania, and that not all Gypsies are Romanian. She said that when she showed the articles in 'Jareeda' to her grandmother, her grandmother was very insulted. Her family is proud to be known as Gypsies. She teaches a workshop on Gypsy skirt dancing, and part of her workshop is teaching the differences between different Gypsy cultures. For instance, a movement that may be acceptable for a Turkish Gypsy to do might be offensive to a Basque Gypsy.

So there is really a lot to this and the controversy goes on. But the dance is passionate and beautiful and fits right in with belly dancing. We love it, and call it Gypsy, Rom or any other name; it smells like a rose to me.

The most recently identified belly dance style is called fusion. Fusion dancing is different dance styles being fused together.

In my competition, we've been doing this for over 20 years. I have a category called Alternative Music which is for the use of alternative music meaning anything but belly dance music. It is a category where dancers blend different dance forms in with belly dancing. For instance, with 20's music they throw in some Charleston movements, with East Indian music they add some Bollywood movements, with country western, they mix in some line dancing, etc.

Fusion is nothing new to me, but it has now hit the dance scene with a force especially in the tribal arena. While there are some things I really like about it, I also have some strong concerns.

What I love about fusion is that it takes us way out of the box, and I love dancing out of the box. It opens up our creativity and expands our abilities in new directions. I love watching a dancer blend African and Indian movements with Middle Eastern dancing. I love the diversity in costumes and music. It makes it fun and interesting to watch as an audience member as well as more fun as a performer to have so many new avenues open to us.

However, the drawback that I see is that many newer dancers grab onto the fusion and emulate or imitate the top fusion dancers in the business without any real training. A parrot can mimic words, but do they really understand language? Can they really communicate? Is a dancer who mimics really a dancer?

My biggest concern about the lack of training is that there can be some serious injuries. The dancers who are making waves by dancing fusion have had years of belly dance training and have expanded their abilities into the area of fusion. They know what they are doing. They were belly dancers first and then fusion dancers.

Some of the new dancers I've seen haven't learned any of the basics of belly dance. They are wearing the costumes, but a costume does not make them a dancer. They need the training first, before they can successfully dance and stay healthy.

Even worse is when I see one of these dancers begin teaching. I know of one who has never had formal lessons who is now teaching. She is a mimic and doesn't really know how to dance, but she has great costumes. I only hope that her students aren't injured and that they don't develop too many bad habits which they will have to change if they want to become serious about their dancing. My hope is the ones who are serious someday find a real belly dance teacher.

Another concern I have regarding different styles, is the "Us against Them" mentality. I mentioned that some Egyptian stylists look down their noses at us 'mere' cabaret dancers, and you don't even want to know what they think about Tribal Style. It isn't 'real' belly dancing is something I used to hear a lot. Now that it's swept the world by storm, it's gaining more and more acceptance. But, the problem is now some tribal dancers are looking down their noses at the Egyptian stylists and cabaret dancers.

I know that it's human nature to want to think that what we are and what we do is better than someone else, but I would love to see belly dancers be more accepting of each other. If we are ever going to heal our planet and find peace among human beings, it has to start somewhere.

Why not start with belly dancers? No matter what our style, we are stepping out of the normal boundaries of our cultures. We are doing something that causes others to judge us either finding fault or fascination. We are all in this together, so let's be supportive of each other and drop the criticism and complaints.

Each of these styles has enriched me as a dancer. Cabaret taught me the basics. Folkloric taught me dances from different countries. Egyptian taught me about control. Tribal taught me tolerance. Gypsy style taught me freedom. Fusion taught me to dance out of the box.

As a member of the audience, I can appreciate each of these styles of belly dance. They each give me something different as I watch them, each make me feel something different, and each gives me different inspirations. It's all belly dancing, and it's all good!

11 TEACHING

After a year of taking lessons, I began to teach. I didn't plan it that way, and I certainly didn't feel qualified to teach. I had taken only one year of lessons, and had performed only four times. The first time in front of class, the second so my teacher could do a quick costume change in a show, the third with my friends and the fourth at the competition where I won second place in the beginner category.

So, I wasn't exactly experienced, and it wasn't my idea to teach, but unfortunately, Katia decided to stop teaching. I never knew why since I really didn't know her personally. All I know is that she stopped teaching, and I wasn't ready to stop learning or stop dancing. I was addicted, totally and completely.

I also practiced 3-6 hours a day, so I was really experienced with the movements I did know, and I had progressed at a rapid rate compared to most dancers.

My friend, Saheena and I began to be approached by people asking us to teach them. After about the 10th person approached us, we talked about it and decided we knew a year more than they did. We decided to start classes and committed ourselves to continue learning, and that's exactly what we did.

Our first class was held in the garage/basement of Saheena's house. We laid down a rug and hung up some Indian bedspreads trying to make it look and feel inviting. We didn't have mirrors, but we taught anyway. I taught the slow movements like hands and arms and undulations, and Saheena taught the fast movements such as hip-work and step combinations.   Together, we made a great team, and our students progressed quickly.

Besides teaching, we also sponsored dancers from Portland to come down to teach on a monthly basis, and we traveled to every workshop and show we heard about within 500 miles.

After about a year, Saheena moved away, and I was left on my own. I continued to teach, and am now known as an expert with special expertise.

Teaching definitely made me a better dancer. As I taught each movement, I learned to break it down and use repetition for my students to learn. The more I did each step, the more I connected with it and felt it in my own body and the better I got.

Teaching also made me a better person. It took me further down the path of coming out of my shell as I became more and more comfortable speaking in front of groups.

As a teacher I became much more aware of people and much more in tune with their needs. I had to learn how to teach in different ways because I discovered that students learn in different ways.

Some students learn by watching me do the movements. They can watch the movement, and then they can do it. I call them visual learners. Others learn by listening to me explain how to do the movement, and I call them audio learners. Others can't figure out what I'm doing by watching or listening. When this happens, I ask them if I can touch them and then I take their arms or hold their hips and gently push and pull them through the movements. I call these dancers kinesthetic learners. Once they feel it in their bodies, they are good to go and can do it on their own.

Not everyone learns in the same way, so I have to be able to help them learn in the way that they need. It's my job, and I've gotten very good at it.

One thing I tell new students is that belly dancing is like learning a new language with our bodies. And I tell them that it's a hard language like learning Russian, but that if they stick with it, they can learn it. Each movement is a new word, and over time the words get easier to learn and soon become sentences, then paragraphs and eventually a whole story as we reach the point of performing.

It isn't easy, and we use muscles we didn't know we had, but we can all do it and do it well if we apply ourselves.

People come to belly dance class for various reasons. Some come because they hear it is good exercise, and they want a more fun workout. Some come because they think it's something exotic, and they feel a bit naughty sneaking out to belly dance class. Some come just because they like to dance, and they've taken modern, jazz and hip hop and belly dance is a new type of dance for them to learn. Some come because their friend wants to do it and doesn't want to go alone.

If a person loves the music and falls in love with the dance, she will become a dancer. She will be beckoned, then compelled, then entranced, then obsessed. She will never want to leave the dance. It either gets into your blood or it doesn't. Amazingly, it's often the friend who got dragged to class that gets bitten by the bug while the friend who does the dragging drops out.

Belly dancing gives us something as women that nothing else seems to give. From what I have observed, it's the students who are missing something in their lives who get hooked. It's also the students who have abusive backgrounds of some type who become hooked, because the dance is a way of healing the wounds they have suffered. It's a dance for women, and class is a safe place and a time-out from the daily stresses of life.

Students who find the movements easy to do, those who come just out of curiosity or because they just want to learn a 'belly dance' for their boyfriend, often don't stay more than a few lessons. The ones who find it easy, usually finds everything easy, and once they learn it they are done and move on to the next class to learn the next thing like putting notches on their belts. "I learned to belly dance once," they tell people later in life. Some women leave because they just can't get past their self-judgment or feelings of inadequacy and some leave because of pressure from their boyfriends or husbands who don't like the changes they see in their 'ol' lady.' Often these same women return months and even years later after their relationship ends.

Women who come to class thinking they will become a belly dancer in six easy lessons so they can dance for their own sultan, usually leave very disappointed. They find that the dance is difficult, not easy and that it may take a lot of practice and lots of lessons to look good enough to even dance for their boyfriend. But, occasionally one of these students becomes intrigued by the dance and becomes hooked.

So whatever reason people come to class, I've learned not to be judgmental. I never know whose passion will be ignited. Out of a new class of 10 people, only 1 or 2 will still be with me in a couple of years. I, myself, was one of those dragged to class by a friend who didn't want to go alone. I can't tell you how many of us are still dancing, after our friends dropped out long ago. It's a hoot!

Other teachers I've talked to have also noticed that it's the students who have personal obstacles to overcome that are more likely to stick with the dance.

One day I was talking to someone about the dance, and she said that we do movements that our mothers always told us not to do, and we laughed. It's so true.

When we dance, we move our hips and our rib cages. We stand up straight and proud with good posture which means our bosoms are sticking out, and then we circle our ribs which make our bosoms circle too. Sometimes we shimmy our shoulders which makes our bosoms move! Oh my!!! And then we sway and shake our hips. How brazen! But, oh, how freeing it feels.

Once, after dancing in a show, a group of women practically mobbed me. They loved my dancing and gave me great compliments, but the best one was, "I just loved how you moved your breasts without inhibition." I knew I had come a very long way from the little girl who was embarrassed of her blossoming breasts.

Many years ago, one of my students developed breast cancer. Miranda first came to me because her first belly dance teacher had suggested she find a new hobby. And, yes, she was awful, but oh did she love the dance. She asked me to please teach her, and I did. It turns out, she was a kinesthetic learner, and when I manually moved her hips, she caught on quickly. She practiced a lot, and before long she was very good. She even won her category in competition, and I was very proud.

When Miranda was diagnosed with breast cancer, we were all devastated, but we all supported her. We were her sisters. She ended up losing her left breast, and we designed special costuming so that no one would ever know anything was missing. We loved her, and she loved us.

She told us a funny story which I will always remember. After her mastectomy, her surgeon told her that she had the most highly developed intercostals he had ever seen. He asked her how she had developed them. For those of you who don't know what intercostals are, they are the muscles between your ribs, one of the sets of muscles we aren't very aware of until we learn to belly dance. So, anyway, she told him she would show him as soon as she recovered and when she was well enough, she belly danced for him, so he could see they type of movements she did to develop those muscles so well. Needless to say, he was impressed.

Unfortunately, we lost Miranda to cancer, but she lives on in each of us who knew her. The night of her wake, my students and I had a dance gig. We all met and talked it over deciding unanimously that Miranda would have wanted us to go, so we did and we dedicated our dances to her. We ended up having one of those hair-raising experiences people talk about.

That night, we all felt Miranda's presence with us, and when Jasmine danced, my first thought was, "What is wrong with her?" Then, I realized that she was dancing exactly like Miranda. There was no mistaking it because she had a very unique way of moving and very different then the way Jasmine danced. It looked like Miranda dancing in her body and was very eerie. After she danced, she said that something weird had happened to her while she was dancing and that she felt weird and didn't remember anything about her dance. We told her that it looked like Miranda dancing and not her, and we all got big Goosebumps. If I hadn't seen it with my own eyes, I wouldn't have believed it. Her young daughter later told us that Miranda was sitting with her during the show. She insisted she saw her and pointed to the chair she sat in. Each of us had felt her presence, and we knew that we had done the right thing by dancing at the show instead of mourning at her wake.

For me, the greatest gift of teaching is my students. Sometimes I feel so low; I can barely force myself to class. If I were just a student, I'm sure on those low days, I would stay home. There is no way I could motivate myself to get to class and I would give in to my depression and wallow. But, since I'm the teacher, I have to be there. I have to drag my depressed butt out the door and on to class.

Because I'm the teacher I have to show up. And, let me tell you: teaching belly dance is the greatest anti-depressant on the planet. I can feel lower than a worm and go to class, teach and leave high as a kite. My students give me what I don't have. They show up full of enthusiasm and eagerness. They are excited about learning, and their excitement is contagious.

One night I was so depressed I actually felt physically ill. I told myself that I could make it through my first class, that I had enough energy for that, and then I could put on a video for my second class to watch and learn from. By the end of my first class, I was so filled with energy that I practically flew through the second class and went home with plenty of energy to burn.

Once, I got in a huge fight with my husband right before the start of a new class session. I was hurt on top of being furious. I have no memory of what the fight was about, but I do remember driving to the college to start a new class wondering how in the heck I was going to do it. How could I possibly stand in front of a new group of people and do a good job when I felt so hurt and angry. And, as I worried about it, I became even angrier at my husband for getting me so upset. I arrived at class and put on a smiling face, a total 'fake it until you make it' moment. In less than five minutes, the enthusiastic questions and eagerness of my new students dissolved my anger into thin air and I came home a happy camper.

Over the years, I have had many students touch my heart, challenge me and give me memories. Most of all, I learn from them as much or more then they learn from me, and I'm a better person for it. Miranda is at the top of the list. She was an inspiration to so many of us.

One of my students became one of my greatest teachers. It was her husband who approached me about her taking lessons thinking it would make her 'sexier.' I suppressed a gag and told him when our next beginner class was, and she showed up. She became captivated by the dance, and she became a member of our first troupe. After almost two years, her husband again approached me. This time he was really angry! He told me that I needed to publish a husband's warning manual and is the one who had told me his wife used to do housework and cook before belly dance and now he had to cook his own dinners. I reminded him that it was his idea for her to take belly dance lessons, and he mumbled something about how I still should have warned him.

The reason this student became such a great teacher for me, is she and my husband fell in love, and I learned so much during that time. Mostly I learned about myself. If I ever had any doubts about what kind of person I was, I learned that I was definitely a good person, and that love was the ruling force of my life. During that time of hell, I maintained my composure and treated both of them with love and kindness. I held my head high despite my shattered heart and found that I was also extremely strong. Their relationship didn't last more than a few months, but what I learned was invaluable. I have never been the same, and I can honestly say that I feel very good about myself as a person and I have more integrity then most people I know. I have absolutely no regrets about how I handled the situation.

Another student who touched me deeply was Juanita. As it turns out, she is the sister of the woman who rocked my world. She was eager to learn and danced for over 25 years until health issues forced her to quit. She was a Goddess of the dance and a joy to anyone who watched her. Juanita and I went on trips to Canada together and other places to dance together. She taught me how to let go more. For example, we once did this dance together where we were supposed to do hip shimmies, then shoulder shimmies. After our performance, a dancer came up to us and said she loved our dance especially the alternating shimmies. I wasn't sure what she was talking about and looked at Juanita. She looked sheepish and told me she had made a mistake and done the shoulder shimmy while I was doing hips and vice versa. The old me would have stressed that she made a mistake. The new me just laughed and told her we were going to start doing that on purpose. I was much more open to new ideas.

Ameena was a student who over time began to out-dance her teacher who was me. I was never threatened but instead proud of her progress and her dedication, but we did end up butting heads as time went by, and I finally encouraged her to teach on her own. She taught me to stand my ground! One time we decided to do a dance together. I thought we'd make a great duet, but we were both too strong headed. Instead of arguing, I stood my ground and told her I wasn't going to dance with her after all. If it wasn't fun, I didn't want to do it and it wasn't fun anymore. I have kept that motto to this day.

My second student who became a professional dancer and teacher was Roxy. Roxy gave me one of my biggest challenges. She came to class so shy, she stood in the back row and was very mousy. She fell in love with the dance and started making up her own routines and costumes. She reminded me more of myself as a beginner than any other student I've ever had. She was in love with the dance. I loved Roxy like a daughter and took her everywhere with me introducing her to all the big names in the business and teaching her everything I knew. Her goal was to be like me and travel and teach workshops, and I was determined to help her reach that goal. Unfortunately, she chose a less positive road, and it became painful to watch her slide away from me, away from her family and away from belly dance.

One of the greatest joys of teaching is watching your students grow and blossom. Sometimes they come to me shy and inhibited. Sometimes they come to me handicapped either emotionally or physically.

Suzanna walked into my class a few years ago with a cane. She'd had a heart attack and a stroke. She had to use a cane because she had balance problems. She couldn't walk backwards, and she definitely couldn't spin. After only 3-4 months, she was able to stop using her cane. She could dance forward and backward, and she could do spins. Her doctor was amazed at her progress telling her he had expected her to be using a cane for the rest of her life. This is one student out of many who have overcome physical obstacles by belly dancing.

And, here's another story about Suzanna. One evening, we struck up a conversation after class. I asked her what she did for a living, and she told me she was a writer. I suddenly realized she was a famous author. She admitted she was, and I let out a squeal. "You're famous! I have several of your books!" She responded that I was famous, too. We had quite a laugh. She is one of the most modest people I've ever met, and has been an inspiration to me. She even dedicated one of her books to me and my dance class. How cool is that?

As a belly dance teacher I feel that my job isn't just to teach dance steps. My job is much more than that. I know what the dance has given me, and I want to give that to my students.

I consider myself a holistic belly dance teacher. I teach my students how to dance and how to costume. I teach them the difference between styles of dance, and I teach them about the culture behind it.

I've worked so hard to gain credibility but potential students often either don't care about teaching credentials or it never occurs to them to ask. They end up with teachers with limited knowledge who don't know the difference between Khaleegy and Hagala, tribal or fusion, etc. It's also frustrating to watch dancers perform who don't know what they are doing. For instance the troupe who did a Saudi woman's dance and wore their Egyptian beledi dresses, not even the same country much less same culture. They didn't know the difference, but other people did and it made them look very unprofessional and their dance would have been insulting to someone from the culture.

Now, don't get me wrong. I'm all for creative expression, and if people want to just dance, that's fine with me. But if they are going to do the dance of a specific culture, then I believe they should educate themselves or offer a disclaimer, such as "Our dance was inspired by…."

One strange thing I've found is that there are some teachers who are only interested in teaching dance class and that's all. In my opinion, if students never perform, their teacher is only half a teacher. To me they are not only lazy, but they are missing one of the best parts of teaching. Nothing can compare to watching your student do her first performance.

A teacher, who only shows up to class once a week, isn't doing her job. It takes an added effort to help students create costuming and to set up performance opportunities, but the reward for that effort is definitely worth it.

I once had a teacher tell me that none of her students were interested in performing, that they were just too shy. I noticed that, not only did they never perform; they never came to any local workshops. When I asked her about that, she said they couldn't afford to take workshops. Now, I've been teaching a really long time, and I really doubt that she has an entire class composed of shy, poor people. Most classes are a mixture of all types of personalities and career choices, and she just wasn't being a good teacher.

I feel strongly that it's my job as a teacher to help shy students overcome that handicap if they want to, and believe me, it is a handicap. As for being too poor, 99% of the time it's priorities and choices, not lack of income that keeps people from attending things. It's my job as a teacher to motivate my students to take advantage of other opportunities to learn besides my classes.

Now, it's wonderful to teach women how to dance. In class, they get in touch with their bodies, get exercise, and they make new friends. It's great to gain a new skill, new body awareness and new friends. My classes are workouts to therapy sessions and everything in between. But learning to dance without ever performing is like getting your driver's license and never driving. What's the point?

On stage is where some real breakthroughs happen. The stage is where we gain our confidence, where we gain raised self-esteem and where we are empowered and strengthened. The stage is where the profound change occurs.

That isn't to say that all students should perform, but I believe that it's my job as a teacher to give my students the option of performing, and to provide them with opportunities to perform. I teach as if everyone is going to perform, giving them information on movements, music, costuming, stage presence, culture and every possible aspect of the dance. I never pressure my students to perform, but I do encourage and make it happen if it's something that they want to do.

We start off with class dances so we all have company on the stage. The really shy dancers are delegated to the back row. We wear very modest costuming to help with the comfort zone, and we do simple dances. Everyone learns the dances in class, and while it isn't a requirement to perform, most people, even the most shy, choose to perform.

As for shyness, do you really know anyone who likes being shy? I certainly don't know of anyone. Belly dancing gave me a chance to beat that demon, and I did it. Was it hard to get on that stage? It was worse than hard; it was terrifying, the most terrifying thing I have ever done on purpose (besides ride my dirt bike down a cliff because the guys were doing it, and I didn't want to look like a wimp.) After performing, I felt euphoric and wanted to do it again. The motorcycle thing? Let's just say it wasn't a confidence builder. I still dance, but the dirt bike is long gone.

The other excuse I hear is, "my students don't perform because they can't afford costuming." Now what kind of excuse is that? Not only do I loan my students simple costuming until they have their own, I teach them how to make costumes using $1 a yard fabric from Walmart if that's all they can afford. If they don't sew, many buy used machines and learn, or I teach them bargain ways to buy and build a costume from pieces found at second hand stores. I've had numerous students, who had never threaded a needle, become amazing costumers. This is another confidence builder, another skill to add to their self-worth.

I've never had a student too poor or too shy to perform. It's part of my job as a teacher to help them overcome their shyness and teach them about costuming. It's my job to teach them how to perform and feel good about it which leads to feeling good about themselves.

My biggest problem with performing students has been with students who come from other dance venues and have already learned to perform. They want to perform, but they don't always want to take the time to learn the art of belly dancing first. With them, my job is to teach them how to belly dance. That isn't always easy when they cling to the movements from other dance forms. There have been times I've had to sit a student down and ask them if they really want to belly dance because from what I'm seeing they want to do jazz or modern dance. Those types of students don't last long.

The opposite also happens. I once had a prima ballerina come to my class, and she was able to let go of her previous discipline and learn how to belly dance. She became a wonderful dancer, and the ballet influence gave her a heads up on posture and stage presence.

I once talked to a teacher who left the studio where she was teaching. Why? The studio owners also sold costumes, and they didn't want her teaching her students how to make their own costuming. This teacher felt like she wasn't able to wholly give the gift of dance to her students, and I understand how she feels.

Learning to dance is fantastic and fun, but performing can be bliss. Performing is what pushes us to grow. When we give our students performance opportunities, it gives them a goal. This goal gives them a reason to get their new costume done, and a reason to practice, practice, practice. It makes them better dancers and better people as they overcome obstacles of self-consciousness and low self-esteem.

Performance is where I watch my students blossom. A teacher, whose students don't perform, misses one of the greatest joys I've had in life, the joy of watching inhibited women, become empowered.

One of my students worked at home, her shyness clearly a handicap. I gave her the option of performing and overcoming that handicap and at one event, she met someone who eventually offered her a job and within two years she was an office manager of a medical clinic! I've had students gain the strength to get out of abusive relationships. I've had students lose lots of weight and students who gain the confidence to make all kinds of positive changes in their lives.

I once had a musician ask me what I did to one of my students. I asked him what he meant and he said, "When I met her, she was a mouse. Now she is proud like a lion!" That was a perfect observation.

I love watching the mouse blossom into a lion. She first comes to class in sweats with no make-up, and she walks hunched with her head down. I always have a stash of hip scarves for my baby students to wear during classes. Before long, the mouse brings her own hip scarf or makes something pretty to go around her hips. She starts to walk with more confidence. But, it's after she begins to perform that her posture lifts up, and her head comes up proudly. She starts to wear make-up and be more aware of her appearance. She takes pride in herself not just as a dancer, but as a woman. She becomes empowered and believes in herself and her abilities. Performance gives her power.

Performing is my gift to my students and their performance is a gift to me. Each dancer has their own unique essence, their own beautiful womanly energy and no one else can ever perform or express in the same way that she can. Every time one of my students performs, I feel as if I have received a beautiful offering.

I have been teaching on-going classes for over 30 years. I have several students who have been with me up to 16 years. If I hadn't moved 17 years ago, the numbers would be even higher. We share the passion of dance.

I also travel and teach workshops around the country, and that is one of my favorite things to do. I love teaching workshops. I meet so many wonderful women around the country, and everywhere I travel, I learn something new, see new things and experience new adventures.

The first workshop I ever taught was in Globe, Arizona. I was visiting my family and was asked to dance in a belly dance show that was happening that week. I did my sword dance, and after I danced, I was swarmed by local dancers who had never seen a sword dance. They asked me if I would teach them a workshop the next day, and I said I would. I had been dancing less than two years, and here I was teaching a large group of women sword dancing. The next year when I visited, I was able to see them perform. They had formed a troupe and did a spectacular dance with swords. It was very heartwarming to see that I had influenced them.

Another workshop highlight was when I taught in Canada. They wanted me to teach double veil, so I brought a lot of extra veils just in case some people didn't have two veils. When I asked people to get out their veils, many of them brought out head scarves. Head scarves? Most veils are at least three yards in length. My first panicked thought was that they didn't even know what a veil was, so that meant they couldn't even do single veil and they wanted me to teach double veil? Yikes! I was so glad to have all those extra veils. First we went over some veil basics, and then we moved on to some simple double veil movements. They were all very happy.

Dancing with double swords.

That evening, I was a guest dancer in their show, and I did double veil and double sword, something I had done many times before. What made this evening different was I received my first standing ovation, with lots of whistling and cheering. I was totally overwhelmed. What a wonderful memory.

When I travel to do workshops, I'm often treated like a star. I'm flown to the location and put up either in a motel or in a person's home and I'm fed and entertained. People even ask for my autograph, and time after time people come up to me saying they have always wanted to meet me. It always makes me feel a bit weird, but it's also really fun. I feel totally humble. Whenever I teach a workshop people are thanking me for the good workshop, and I'm thanking them for inviting me. It's a two way street.

I know that some dancers get a big head and act like they deserve to be treated like a queen, but I am just so happy and grateful to have the opportunity to travel and teach. I love teaching, and I love making new friends!!

And, one last point about teaching is that I will always be a student of the dance. My learning never ends because belly dance is so rich with diversity and endless facets of information that I will never be able to learn it all!

12 CAREER

So, I started teaching after only a year of lessons. It's not something I recommend, but it's how I got started. I was extremely dedicated and I spent many hours a day practicing and drove thousands of miles to continue my education. I've always taught from the heart and have never made much money beyond the cost of space rental, but I can't imagine not teaching.

After I began teaching, I also started doing what we called 'Belly Grams.' Just like a singing telegram, I was hired to surprise people with a belly dance. I mostly danced at birthday parties and a few retirements.

When someone called for a belly gram, I would help them plot the surprise. It was often in a public place such as a restaurant and I would ask for a description of the recipient, would arrange to have someone meet me at the door and carry in my boom box and then I would dance into the room and surprise the person receiving the gram.

I made over $400 a month doing these which was really good money in the early 80's, and it was a very fun way to earn money.

One of my recipients was a Dr. and I danced for him at our local hospital in a meeting room. As I danced, he noticed my gall bladder scar and asked, "Did you get that here?"

Everyone laughed including me as I replied, "Yes, I did!"

Another belly gram was for a singer arranged by his band members. They asked me to dance for him after he performed his solo, and he had to act cool as the audience watched his response to my dance. He said over the microphone, he didn't know where to look!

Once I danced for Santa in the middle of the mall in front of a huge crowd, and another time a guy panicked and ran from the room. Then there was the time I was asked to do a gram at a bank in a tiny town near where I lived. The receiver was described as a man with bright red hair in a suit. Imagine my surprise to dance into the bank and see two men with bright red hair in suits. I wasn't sure who to aim for and fortunately one of the tellers pointed him out.

Most of the victims, I mean recipients, were initially embarrassed then thrilled with the attention. I was never flirty, just had fun with everyone in the room, often dancing at family parties. It was always a blast, and my business grew through word of mouth. After a few years, several dancers in my area began doing belly grams, and business decreased.

Next, I started vending as a way to 'pay for my habit.' I never had a surplus of money with my regular jobs, making only what I needed to pay bills and eat. So if I wanted to travel and dance, I had to find a way to pay for it, so I started selling things. First it was beaded earrings and necklaces. Then I made a few more things. I made just enough to pay my expenses and to shop or trade for that next costuming item or dance accessory.

Before I ever started vending on my own, I traveled with my friend, Halima and helped her vend. I helped her unload and set up her tables, then sell, then pack up and load it all back up. She would let me sell my beaded earrings at her table, and then I'd spend the money I made on supplies from her. For years, that's how I paid for all my costuming supplies.

Halima and I had a great time together, and on one of our very long trips we headed to Salt Lake City for their annual belly dance festival. We traveled in her husband, Bud's truck, and had all kinds of troubles. First the truck kept losing water and overheating. This was a very large four wheel drive Dodge Ram pick-up and we kept having to stop and Halima would get out a step ladder which she needed to reach the hood. Then she'd climb up and open the hood and we would pour water in. Sometimes we had a water source such as a hose at a gas station, and sometimes it was Pepsi cups full of water. On that trip we also broke off his antennae, and crunched his KC lights on top of the cab going through an underground parking garage below the motel. It was a disastrous trip for that poor truck, and Bud was so gracious about the whole thing.

When we got to Salt Lake City, it was an outdoor festival which meant setting up and breaking down every day. By the time we were done, we were totally exhausted. On the drive home we had more adventures, and Halima told me she was doing too much in her life and that she needed to let something go. She decided that she loved her costuming business and that she needed to let go of her magazine, '*Jareeda.*' I immediately told her that I wanted it, and she tried to talk me out of it. She said it was too much work, but as soon as she said she was letting it go, I knew I had to have it. It just felt right inside. I loved to write, and here was a chance to channel another passion into my life. What could be better than combining my love for writing with my love for dance?

So, she finally agreed, and for the rest of the long hours home, she told me how to run the magazine in as much detail as possible. I asked her a gazillion questions, and I filled a whole notebook full of notes.

January 1994 was my very first issue. I was excited and relieved all at the same time. In one month I went from knowing nothing about computers or publishing to buying a computer and learning how to run a publishing program. I had no money to buy a computer, but I had a friend who offered to loan me the money I needed; he was an angel.

So, I had my computer and then I had to learn how to use it. Fortunately my daughter, Avena, who was in eighth grade at the time, knew about computers; she was a huge help. I used to get so frustrated! I'd get lost somewhere in my computer and wouldn't be able to find my way back. I would yell, "Avena, help!" And, she would come and rescue me. With her aid I learned computer basics. I remember at one point, I fantasized about throwing my computer out the window and into the blackberry bushes behind my home. Now when I think back, I can't believe I found it so difficult, but I did.

I was told that Microsoft Publisher was the most user friendly program, so that is what I bought. Being completely computer illiterate, I was able to learn how to put the magazine together on a computer with no cutting and pasting and do it in less than a month while working full-time and being a single mom of two children, a teen and a toddler. Yes, I felt pretty amazing but I didn't get much sleep that month.

When I first took over *Jareeda* it was a monthly magazine, but within two years I found it impossible to keep up with that schedule. It was mostly a labor of love, so I still had to work a full-time job, and I cut it back to eight issues a year. Eight issues were still more than any other belly dance publication out on the market. *Jareeda* is going through another big transition, and I'm working on a kindle edition. Woo Hoo!

I love my magazine. I have met so many wonderful people over the years through *Jareeda*, and experienced so much. Most of my experiences have been good, but a few haven't been so good. One problem I had for awhile was that I had a hard time separating myself from my magazine. There were a few times I thought people wanted to be friendly to me, but what they really wanted was to be in the magazine. It was really just butt kissing, but I was too naïve to see that. I didn't understand at the time that owning a magazine apparently have me some prestige in their minds. Now, I know the difference.

It's interesting being the publisher of a magazine. I once had a dancer come up to me and ask me why I had never asked her to be on the cover of *Jareeda*. She asked me if I was unfriendly, or what? I paused for a few seconds searching for words, and then I told her. I told her that I was very friendly, and she could ask anyone about that, and that many years before when I was a baby dancer, I had approached her to ask her a question. She looked down her nose at me and said, "You are talking to me, why?" And then she turned and walked away.

When I told her about this, she admitted that she did have a hard time being friendly. I told her that I didn't have any hard feelings or hold any grudges, but it had just never occurred to me to approach her again.

I always tell people that story as an example of how important it is to be nice to everyone. You never know who in your life might someday be in a position to give you a hand up.

I've had so many people tell me that what I said to them changed their lives. Sometimes I have no memory of who they are, or maybe just a vague inkling, and I never remember what I said. I just know that it's important to always speak with loving intent, to reach out when people are hurting and to lend a helping hand when needed.

Jareeda is still a labor of love. Unlike other publications, I focus my energy more on getting quality article content and less energy on getting advertising. Advertising is where the money is, but I personally like to read good articles. I have picked up other belly dance publications that have 2-3 articles and page after page of advertising! I want *Jareeda* to have some substance, and since my energy is limited I make less money than I could because I want my magazine to be reader friendly.

I also want *Jareeda* to be a magazine for everyone, and I publish articles by contributors from all over. Some publications go for the 'big names' in the business, but *Jareeda* includes everyone from beginner to big name. As a reader, I like hearing what dancers are doing around the world, not just in my backyard. I love personal interest stories, so my favorite articles are the ones telling about how belly dancing changes lives, or about the adventures dancers have.

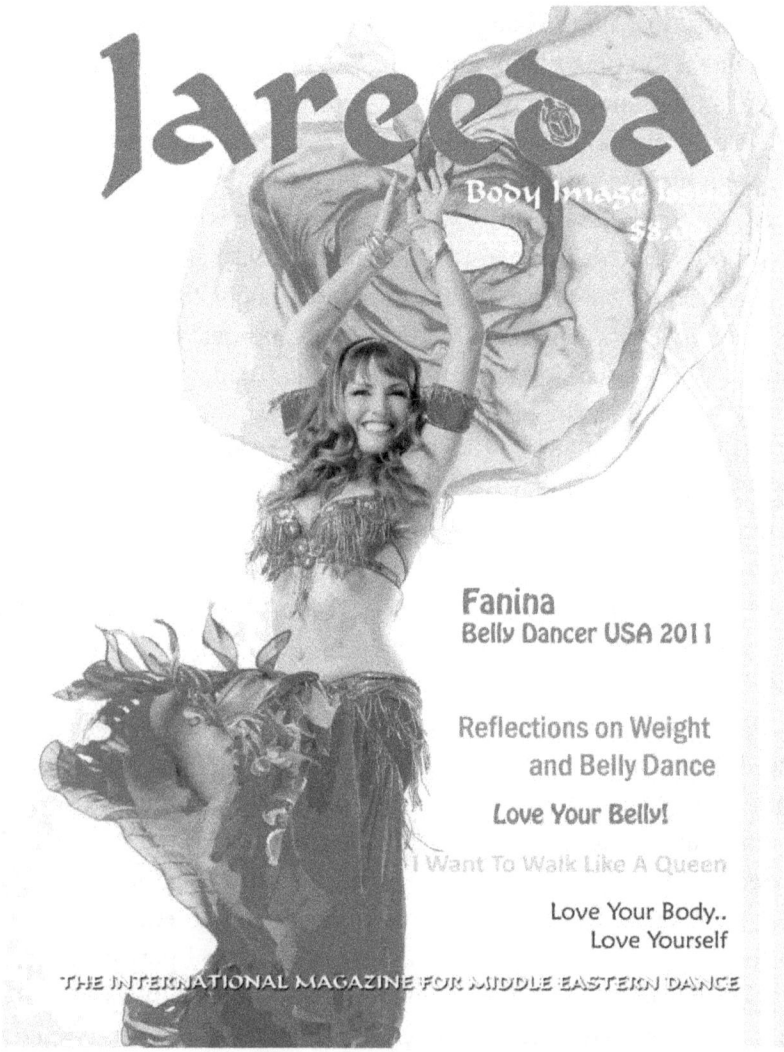

Jareeda

Body Image Issue
$8.00

Fanina
Belly Dancer USA 2011

Reflections on Weight
and Belly Dance

Love Your Belly!

I Want To Walk Like A Queen

Love Your Body..
Love Yourself

THE INTERNATIONAL MAGAZINE FOR MIDDLE EASTERN DANCE

Also, people tend to think of *Jareeda* as having a staff. The true reality is that I am the staff. At times I have students help me with mailings, but I do all lay out, all the correspondence, etc.

I do have wonderful staff writers and contributors, who send me most of the content, and believe me when I say email is a life enhancer. I used to receive typewritten articles that I had to scan into the computer. Then I had to use OCR (optical character recognition) software so that I could edit the articles, all before inserting them into the lay out. Now I receive almost everything either in emails or as email attachments which saves many long hours.

When I moved to Sutherlin, Oregon a tiny redneck town, I was soon able to stop working my day job and focus more on *Jareeda* and teaching. It was like a dream come true. I know that many people aren't able to work at what they love so I know that I am truly blessed.

One of my dreams was to open my own dance studio, and I was also able to do that in 2000. My friend Tara Anya and I rented an old cement block building which had been used as an auto garage. It had two big garage doors and was ugly with a capital U! We put down rugs over the cement floor, and draped tapestries and veils around, put up some mirrors and created what our 'men' called, 'girl space.' I called it 'Mystical Oasis Dance Studio,' and it was a true oasis, a place for us to get away from the everyday humdrum to dance and laugh. The rent was cheap because it had no water or bathroom. My landlord was an attorney, and he let me have a key to his office so that we could use his bathroom whenever we needed. So when one of us needed to potty, we said we were going to consult our attorney. Those were the days!

The building had a heater, but it was a very small heater, and the building was very large, so we had to dance fast in the winter to stay warm. There was no air conditioning, so in the summer we danced slowly on those hundred degree days. We had several fans going, but it was still very, very hot. None of us really cared because we just loved to dance!

There was a 20'X30' suspended loft, and that was my office and where I worked on the magazine. After a couple of years, I moved my computer home. It seemed like I was gone 24/7, and I felt the need to be home and more accessible to my son, so the loft became more of a storage unit.

A few years later, my ex and I bought our own building and I moved the studio there. The payments were more, of course, but we had a bathroom and air conditioning which was a boon for my health, and it was all ours. The building was bigger than our house. The studio was in the back of the building, and was so beautiful. It was much smaller than the auto garage, but I loved it. The old studio was all cement block, and I couldn't hang my pictures up, but this one had a big wall that I covered with beautiful papyrus paintings and other belly dance art. The energy there was wonderful.

In the front of the building, facing the main street in town, we opened a rock and gem store, and a belly dance boutique. It also had a good-sized room for my office which I filled with my treasures and shelves of *Jareeda* back issues. It was totally me.

At the time we also owned a restaurant. I used to joke that we had to buy a restaurant so we'd have a regular place to perform. For years, we danced there on the first and third Thursdays at 6 p.m. It gave us a great venue to try out our new routines, and our dancing helped bring in revenue for the restaurant, a win-win situation.

I'll never forget our first performance there. After assuring our customers that belly dancing was family entertainment, the place was packed out. I danced around the room interacting with each person and at one point stopped and shimmied at one of the tables. As I shimmied, my skirt dropped to the floor!

I was mortified! Horrified! I had harem pants under the skirt and a beladi dress on top of it, but still! I stepped out of my skirt and exited to the kitchen. I told my husband who was trying not to fall on the ground laughing along with the whole room of diners, "We are selling the place. I can never show my face here again!" But, of course, I danced there dozens of more times over the years.

During my divorce, the ex got the restaurant, and we lost our regular gig. I got the rock shop and dance studio. Within a few months, the restaurant was closed, and I can truthfully say it couldn't make it without my management. He was the best cook in the county, but I was the one with a head for numbers and business.

After a few years, I closed my store, one of the best decisions I ever made. With the help of my students, I created a studio on my property, transforming the dirty, greasy, garage-rock shop into a true oasis. It's like walking into another world and the best studio yet. The energy is amazing, and we absolutely love it!

My studio lives on and I have more students than ever. I love being able to share my passion!

Once I started teaching workshops, people started asking me if I had any videos. So that was my next career project. My daughter and I produced several videos. The first one was called 'Veiled Visions' and was everything I knew at the time about single veil, double veil and capes and included some performances by myself and Avena. The next video we produced was called 'Balancing Act' which was about balancing and dancing with props, especially single and double sword. Next was a video called, 'Hypnotic Hands and Arms,' about what else but hands and arms. Then, I put out beginner and intermediate videos which covered all aspects of the dance including steps, veil work, floor work and finger cymbals. The last one I produced was called Competition Savvy which was the very first video to be produced for dancers interested in competing.

Now when I vend, I sell my magazine, my videos, music and the jewelry I make. I started making jewelry because belly dancers buy costuming and jewelry first and magazine subscriptions last. They usually pick up a subscription form at events and mail it in later, so I needed something to make money with at events, and jewelry was the perfect thing.

So between teaching weekly classes, teaching seminars, selling my videos and publishing *Jareeda*, I have a career as a belly dancer. Now what other form of dance could an overweight, middle-aged woman make a living dancing as a teacher and performer? I've been blessed with so many friends to support me over the years helping me to be successful. There is nothing like belly dance!

13 PUBLIC SPEAKING

When I first started going to class, I was shy, but my teacher was easy to be around and I got used to the other students. The dance felt good in my body and this was something I needed and wanted. I loved it.

As I explained earlier, belly dance gave me confidence, and it helped my self-esteem. Here was finally something I excelled at. My first competition was a real eye-opener. It opened up my world. I was no longer a tiny fish in a tiny pond; I was a tiny fish in a huge ocean. There were belly dancers everywhere! And, I wanted to learn what they knew.

In those days, learning to belly dance wasn't easy. There was no such thing as videos. Teachers were few and far between. My teacher quit teaching after I'd had less than a year of lessons, and I began to teach because there was such a demand. Now I cringe when I hear of people teaching after less than a year of lessons, but I was lucky to have a teacher who taught wisely and emphasized safety. She knew what she was doing, and I followed in her footsteps. I didn't go my own way, but continued what she was doing.

I needed to keep learning myself, so I looked for workshop opportunities. Currently, I can find a workshop almost every weekend, sometimes more than one within a 100 mile range. In those days, I was lucky to find one every few months at a distance of at least 400 miles. I had to drive to either Seattle or San Francisco to find workshops. Sometimes I had students with me and sometimes I went alone. My compulsion to learn, strongly overcame my fear of driving.

Sometimes workshop opportunities actually came to Portland, a mere

225 miles away. That was always a bonus. I also started bringing teachers to Coos Bay from Portland on a monthly basis for my students to also learn from.

As I traveled, I began to make friends, and I became more and more known in the belly dance community. I competed in contests, a major accomplishment for my shy self, and I was asked to dance in major shows throughout the Northwest.

Dancing was one thing, but public speaking was another. When I danced, I had on a costume, and it was like putting on the cloak of a different part of me, one that was separate from my everyday self. Mezdulene was outgoing and social, but I wasn't. Over time, I became Mezdulene, but in the beginning it was like having two personalities. It sounds weird, but I think it was the only way I could have gotten onto that stage. I've heard other entertainers talk about the same thing, how on screen or performing they are one way, but privately they are very shy. I could certainly relate.

One day, very early in my career, I showed up with my students at a big gig. We were dancing for some sort of benefit in front of a huge crowd. After we danced, the emcee came up and said, "Tell us some of the history of belly dancing," and he handed me the microphone. I have no idea what I said, but I do remember the feeling of terror, and I have a vague memory of stuttering and lots of ums and uhs. I felt like an idiot!

I learned something that day. People didn't just want to watch us perform; they were also interested in knowing about the dance. So, I wrote up a brief history of the dance and started taking it with me whenever we danced. I practiced in front of a mirror a few times, and it wasn't long before I had it memorized. Many, many times I've had people thank me and tell me that belly dancing wasn't at all what they had previously thought it was and they were glad to know more about it.

I started to use every occasion we danced as an opportunity to educate the public about my art form. I have found that most dancers don't do this which is very unfortunate. Most of them are afraid of public speaking just like I was, and they don't understand the importance of educating the public. For instance, my ex mother-in-law hates when I pick up the microphone. She just wants to dance and thinks it's a waste of time but since I moved to the area, education has increased our dance opportunities. My introduction is under 2 minutes long, and I encourage all dancers to take every opportunity to educate about our art form and dispel any fantasies or misconceptions.

This is the gist of what I say, sometimes longer sometimes shorter. Feel free to use it yourself.

"Belly dancing is the oldest dance form dating back thousands of years to the time of Mother Goddess worship when women were revered for their life-giving ability. (Depending on the crowd, I sometimes add, 'this is before they knew men had anything to do with it. I've gotten lots of laughs with that one!) Our dance is a verbal and visual tradition passed down through the generations from mother to daughter. In America, we take steps from countries throughout the Middle East and put them together creating our own form of Middle Eastern Dance. Belly dancing isn't limited to the young and agile like many dance forms. Anyone can belly dance, any age or any size. I've had students from age 3 to age 88. Belly dancing was done by women, for women for thousands of years and was brought into the public view only a couple of hundred years ago. The movements we will be doing today, when we perform, are the same movements our sister dancers have done for thousands of years and the same movements our sisters will be doing thousands of years into the future. These movements are the same movements that our sisters are doing all around the planet in almost every country. Belly dancing gives us a link to other women throughout time and space. Today we will be presenting a variety of cabaret and folkloric dances, and we hope that you enjoy the show. Feel free to clap along with the music. The dancers enjoy your feedback."

My students have heard this over and over, but every audience has new members who have never seen belly dancing before, or have no idea of the history or a tainted idea of the history.

Another thing that should be announced is a brief explanation of dances that are different, either in costuming, culture or comedy, and sometimes I even teach audiences how to zaghareet.

Here is what happens when dance groups don't speak and educate their audience. I had some new beginners who went to watch another dance troupe in our area. There was no announcing, and my students came to me with several questions. Fortunately I was familiar with the routines. One of them is a comedy dance that uses all the moves you shouldn't ever do, but my students didn't know it was comedy and neither did the audience. It was meant to be tacky, and all in fun, but without an announcement it was just plain tacky to those who weren't in the know and disturbing for my new students.

Other groups don't agree with my policies, but I've found that announcing has been very beneficial. When I first moved to Sutherlin, I still ran into many people who thought belly dancers were just bar dancers and this was after years of belly dancers in the area dancing without adding the educating piece.

I do things differently and because of it, my studio is well-respected in our community.

Another thing I do differently is, when we dance outdoors, I make it a rule for all dancers to be completely covered. When people see us at a distance in a park where they can't hear our music, they just see us undulating and shimmying with our bellies exposed which feeds into their preconceived notions of hootchy kootchy. In fact, a big hoity toity local art festival banned local belly dancers after their performance but I was able to get a spot for my dancers because of my professionalism. At outdoor events, many people see us who wouldn't normally buy a ticket to a belly dance show, so festivals are a big opportunity to educate.

It's my opinion that we need to be as discreet as possible in these types of venues to prevent any more alienation of the public than we already might have. I also don't dance in bars and don't let my students dance in bars or at stag parties. I constantly advertise that we are family entertainment, and I bring little girl students to as many events as possible. I am in people's faces educating and volunteering to perform for good causes, and I haven't had an ignorant comment in years now.

I have spoken and done dance demonstrations at Lion's clubs and other organizations. Organizations are always looking for interesting public speakers. I became a minister and do weddings and memorials. I no longer have trouble with public speaking, a long way from the person who uhmmed and ahhed when handed the microphone many years ago.

A few years ago, I took a personality test given by a counselor. He told me I was in 1/2 of 1 percent of the population. He said I was off the chart when it came to introversion. I told him I used to be introverted but felt more like an extrovert now. He told me the personality doesn't change. He said, "You're still an introvert but with a highly expanded comfort zone." I've always remembered that remark. It was so true.

14 PROFESSIONALISM

I've been asked many times about professionalism over the years, and in my opinion, there are several facets to being professional.

Because I have taught for more than 30 years, travel and teach seminars, have instructional DVDs, publish *Jareeda*, an international belly dance publication, there is no doubt that I am a professional in my field.

For some, however, being a 'professional' belly dancer merely means dance ability and costuming. We have competitions, such as my own contest, Belly Dancer USA, that have many categories from beginner to professional.

The criteria for entering the professional category are simple. Anyone who promotes or advertises themselves as a teacher or professional belly dancer can enter this category. Or, in other words, if you want to compete and you are a teacher or you promote yourself as a professional, you 'have to' enter this category.

Over the past thirty years, the quality of dancing has increased and the technique has become much more intricate and demanding. What passed as a professional level performer in 1980 would no longer be considered professional in the present.

When I was in the competition circuit, I competed as a beginner the first year and because I started teaching, I had to compete in the professional category the second year. I hold firm to this rule in my own contest. I had to do it, and so does anyone who teaches. If you aren't a professional, then what qualifies you to teach?

Now, I know I said I didn't feel qualified to teach when I started, but I did it, and I continued to take as many workshops as possible and practiced several hours a day. So, when I entered the professional category in my second year of dance, I held my own. I didn't win, but I held my own. In my third year of competing I won second place in the professional category.

Dancers who enter the professional category consider themselves professionals, but not all of them are professional in my opinion.

I believe there is much more to being a professional dancer then just advertising that you are or teaching, but for competition there is really no other way to filter without becoming too complicated.

If your job is belly dancing, in other words, you make your living by belly dancing, than you are most likely a professional. Otherwise, you wouldn't be able to make a living doing it.

That being said, here is what I consider criteria for professionalism.

Commitment: Being committed to being the best dancer you can be by continuing to learn, to take classes and to practice.

I know one teacher who considers herself a professional. She came to my retreat for a number of years and never took even one of the ten workshops offered. Why? Because she was a teacher, so she already knew everything and she certainly didn't want anyone to think she needed to take a class. What she didn't know is that she has lost a lot of respect in the dance community with that attitude, and she still dances like she never left the 80s. She enters competition after competition and has no clue why she doesn't win because she practices a lot. Yes, she practices a lot, but she is stuck in the past where technique was much less intricate. If she continued to educate herself, she would have been a top professional in the field long ago.

Costuming: It's important to wear a professional quality costume that fits well and compliments the dance.

I once had a student who had great technique. When it came to her dancing, she was professional level and she decided to enter the professional category at a competition. Her costume was not professional quality. I tried to advise her, but she refused to listen to me. She didn't place and decided it was because she was too fat. A few years later, she decided to enter a different contest and again, her costume wasn't up to par, and again she didn't want to listen to me. I reminded her that a contest could be won or lost by just one or two points and asked her if she was willing to lose costuming points. That got her attention. She did what I advised and won second place in a very prestigious competition.

I also knew a dancer with very large breasts who costumed to show them off and a dancer with severe scarring on her belly from childbirth and surgery who refused to wear a belly cover. People didn't remember them by their dancing; they remembered the dancer with the big boobs and the dancer with the scarred belly. When there is a glaring physical feature, or costuming flaw such as a too small bra or crack showing belt, the eye is drawn to that and it's hard to focus on the dance.

Simply put, a professional dancer knows how to costume to compliment her dance, not distract from it.

Teaching: The desire to share the dance from the heart.

I know many professional belly dancers who teach but who aren't able to dance with the caliber of technique that we see winning contests today. This doesn't make us less professional.

In fact, I once took a workshop from an amazing dancer. She was an excellent teacher, was able to break down the steps when needed and she had a great sense of humor and kept us riveted and wanting more. Later, when she danced, I was amazed at her awkwardness.

I have also taken workshops from great performers who couldn't teach their way out of a tissue paper bag.

A great teacher is not always a great performer and a great performer is not always a great teacher, but they can both be professionals.

I'll tell you a funny story about me. I was at a show and sitting next to another instructor. My student was dancing and this instructor leaned over and whispered, "She's great! I wonder who her teacher is?" I replied that I was her teacher. She looked surprised and said, "But she has such great technique!" I told her that just because I didn't dance it didn't mean I didn't teach it!

And there is my friend Halima, one of the most respected professionals in the business who can't dance at all due to becoming handicapped. But she is still a great teacher and knows more about the dance than almost anyone else I know.

Attitude: Having a positive attitude on stage and off.

I belief that as professionals, it's important that we set an example by being the best person we can be whether we are performing or just attending an event.

Having a professional attitude is not about ego as some mistake it to be; it's about doing a good job and being supportive of all dancers whether they are beginners or other professionals. It's about having a positive impact in our dance community and setting a good example. It's about being grateful for opportunities and so much more.

I once had a student who thought she was a professional and no longer needed me as her teacher. Her problem was that in leaving the nest she found it necessary to become snotty and disrespectful towards me. Because of that, she lost all credibility in the dance community. She was a shooting star full of ability and expertise, but she crashed to the earth because of her attitude.

Then there was the colleague who bad mouthed me in our community at large. Now, locally, my reputation is stellar and she just made herself look bad when she did it around here. But, here is an example of an epic fail on her part. I was asked by a sponsor to teach a workshop in another state along with a really big named belly dancer. The big name taught on Saturday, and I taught on Sunday. When I got there, I had much fewer sign-ups which is normal for being a 'little' name and teaching on Sunday. However, after seeing me dance in the show, several more people signed up for my workshop and I actually ended up with a larger turnout than the big name.

Later the sponsor confided in me that my colleague had told her I wouldn't be a good draw and that she had invited me anyway because she liked me personally. Then she went on to say that when my colleague taught there she only had six people in her workshop.

I've heard similar things about this person and others like her along with the statement "I'll never have her back and I won't recommend her to other sponsors." This particular dancer is a good teacher, but she shot herself in the foot with her bad attitude.

Respect: Give the respect to others that you want to receive yourself. This is actually another aspect of attitude, but I think it's an important one to clarify.

This one seems like a big, duh! I wish that were true, but unfortunately, it's not.

There are the diva dancers who want others to look up to them and

113

respect them and even act as if we should bow down to them, but they don't give baby dancers the time of day and don't respect their colleagues. On stage, they are wonderful dancers and seem very professional, but off stage they are just plain self-centered and egotistical.

Dancers like this show up to dance but don't stay to support their fellow performers. They just put in an appearance, and they miss so much. Their attitude seems to say, they are too good to mingle with the peasants.

Because of this, they miss out on the sisterhood of our dance. If they try to teach, their students don't last long because of their condescending attitude.

I was once begged by the mom of one of these diva dancers to ask her daughter to teach at my retreat. I agreed, and I had more complaints about her one hour workshop then I'd had in the other fifteen years put together. I was told she was stuck up, condescending, put people down, acted like they were stupid, etc. It was awful. She didn't respect her students, and they certainly didn't respect her. It's a sad story, but true.

Another form of respect is self-respect. This is a very important part of professionalism. If I don't respect myself as a professional, I can't expect anyone else to respect me as one.

Many years ago when my students and I first started dancing in the community, we were thrilled about any opportunity to dance. We got several festival gigs which came with some issues. One of the issues is that the band was always paid, but we were always expected to donate our time. I was okay with that because it was an opportunity to dance, got us out into public view and was a great way to educate about our art form and gain new students. However, if there was a delay, we were the ones asked to wait. One year we were left standing in the smoke of barbequed tuna at the Charlie Tuna Festival, waiting and waiting. The next year, they did it again. They were running behind and the so and so band needed to go on during our time slot, could we please wait? I knew we were their biggest draw and I also knew they weren't respecting me, so I very nicely said, no, we couldn't wait. We either needed to dance at the time we prepared for, or we had to leave because we had somewhere else we needed to be. Oh my! Suddenly we were dancing on time!

Another time we were asked to dance at a huge show celebrating the

85th anniversary of a local vaudeville theater. They asked me specifically to dance with my snake and asked for my students to also perform a few dances. The fly in the ointment was I had to come up with sheet music because all the music in the show was going to be played on the old pipe organ. That was cool, not easy, but I did it. I contacted John Bilezikian and paid him to write me some sheet music.

There were several rehearsals and at each rehearsal our time was cut which meant revising our performances. After the third time cut, I was getting cranky, but when I was told we weren't professional enough because we didn't have our act together in rehearsal, I blew my top.

I told the big time Broadway producer that I had performed in shows from San Francisco to Victoria, Canada to Egypt and that he was the least professional producer I had ever had the displeasure of working with, that he cut our time every rehearsal which meant we had to revise our dances on the spot and that as professionals, we were no longer interested in being a part of such an unprofessional event.

Presto chango! Immediately we became the most important performance in the show, and the guy was practically leaving hickeys on my butt he was kissing so hard. I told him I'd give him another chance, and we were treated like queens the rest of the time and received the best reviews of the show. Of course we did!

In summary, professionalism is about commitment to continue to learn and grow in the dance, wearing appropriate costuming, teaching from the heart, having a positive attitude and treating others and ourselves with respect.

So, if you want to be considered a pro, act like one!

15 COMPETITION

Many dancers don't believe in competitions; they've never entered one and most have never even attended a contest.

Everyone has their own opinion, but I'd like to suggest that before you eliminate competing from your agenda, you at least consider attending one as an audience member.

I started Belly Dancer USA out of the desire to help other dancers expand their own comfort zones. While I've sponsored many events over the years, workshops, shows and my retreat, my competition is the most brutally time-consuming and life-sucking event of all and yet it's very rewarding. Almost every year I say I'm not going to do another one and by the end of the weekend, I'm planning the next year. It's crazy!

When you sponsor a workshop and show, you rent a space, invite someone to teach, ask people to dance in the show, invite vendors and advertise. You may or may not have live music and you need a music system and lighting. Then you sign people up for the class and when the date arrives you set up the stage and facilitate the event.

For Belly Dancer USA, I do all the same stuff but on top of it, we have to collect prizes for 1st, 2nd and 3rd place in eleven categories, buy trophies, get a crown, make sashes, make certificates and recruit good judges.

It's a Herculean task that takes up many, many hours of my time before the date of the event. Back in the late 90's I almost quit, almost gave it up because it was just too much. My students stepped up to the plate and promised to help, so I kept at it. Today, the contest runs like a well-oiled machine thanks to the help of my students who are also my friends. When it comes to competitions, I believe we set the standard. That isn't ego talking, it's from feedback, 30 years of producing BDUSA and my experience attending and judging other competitions.

I get so many comments about how smoothly things go, and what a great experience it was, how lovely the stage looks, or wonderful dressing room and my wonderful stage manager, and they love my stories when I MC. This list goes on! My favorite thing is when a dancer tells me how much it opened up her world, or how helpful the score sheets and judge comments are or what a sisterhood they experienced back stage. This is what keeps me working so hard to create this event.

Another really positive aspect of competition is the audience draw. When I sponsor a workshop and show, I'm lucky to sell a few tickets, and I've gone financially in the hole more than once.

My contest is a huge audience draw and I've never lost money putting it on even with the added expenses. People seem to be fascinated by contests; the public is attracted by droves. It gives us a great opportunity to educate the public about our art form, and it attracts lots of belly dance enthusiasts and belly dancers who don't compete, but love to watch and support dancers who do.

My own competition experience opened my world in ways I never could have imagined. While I didn't always win, I was seen by sponsors and asked to dance in their shows. I gained popularity as a direct result of competing. I mentioned earlier dancing to George Abdo, singing. I also got to dance with The Sultans the band that Omar Faruk Tekbileck started in and with many other great bands.

I encourage everyone who is serious about their art form to compete and even made a DVD and teach a workshop titled Competition Savvy. I don't think competing is for everyone, but it is for those who are truly serious about their dance, those who want to overcome stage fright, those who want to get feedback from professionals in the field so that they can learn more about where they excel and what they need to work on and those who want to push themselves to do the very best they can do.

Competition isn't for dancers who are just dancing for fun or those who don't care whether or not they improve. It's not for dancers who think they already know everything, and it's not for dancers with big egos.

It isn't easy to dance on a stage with judges sitting at tables in front of a large audience, but there is nothing more motivating! If for nothing else, I advocate competing because of the motivation. It gives dancers a goal to work towards and gives them the drive to practice, and to be the best that they can be.

My contest is a safe environment for dancers. Whether they compete only once in their career or chose to compete repeatedly, competition is a healthy way for dancers to grow and get better at what they do if they have the right attitude.

What is the right attitude you may be wondering? The right attitude is to do the best you can. The wrong attitude is to do it to win.

Dancers with the right attitude win whether or not they get a trophy. Here are some testimonials from dancers who have competed in Belly Dancer USA and didn't win a trophy:

"This was my first competition and it was a wonderful experience. In this instance you certainly succeeded in making it the growing experience that you hope to share with us newer dancers. Thanks so much for putting this on and taking such pains to make the score sheets helpful. You offer a great competition experience at a nice hotel and I thoroughly enjoyed myself. Thank you."

"I would like to thank you for putting on the Bellydancer U.S.A. competition, because I learned some of the most important tips over this weekend. I was so unprepared for what I was about to find at this event. I was surprised to find, and meet, some of the nicest women I have ever met. I was half expecting to find some over-inflated egos, and attitudes, but I was really shocked when I didn't run into that at all. This is my first experience at a competition, ever. I wanted to say, I felt very welcome, and almost like a part of a sisterhood, all of the dancers backstage, cheered each other on, and were so kind and encouraging to one another. I think everyone was a winner for that reason. Thank you for a memorable experience!"

"I've recently arrived home to Washington from the Bellydancer USA competition this past weekend. It was also nice to see how complimentary and appreciative you were to all who helped you, the vendors, and even the audience. I also didn't get the usual "ego" that I find when dealing with dancers who have been in the business for a long time. No one there came off with pompous airs, and I really appreciated that. The atmosphere all weekend long was so pleasing; it made the entire 18 hour drive well worth it! So thank you for your incredibly hospitality."

These are just a few notes from people who didn't win, but as you can see they also didn't lose. I believe that any dancer who puts herself out there in a competition is a winner and already a step above those who let fear hold them back from succeeding.

Over the years I have seen a few dancers with the wrong attitude who shouldn't be competing. These are the dancers with the huge egos who think they already know it all and think they are the best. When they don't win, it has to be the judge's fault because in their mind they are the best so they didn't need to practice and prepare. Fortunately these are very few and far between, but here are a couple of stories.

One time my student, Juanita, won first place in her category. She was the best dancer that day, right on the mark. I was so proud. Imagine my distress when I heard this story later. One of the other competitors yelled at Juanita in the dressing room saying that she should have won first because, she was the best dancer, not Juanita. Juanita was so upset; she offered the woman her trophy. Another of my students jumped in and told the woman that she needed a reality check. She didn't even get third place, didn't place at all and that she didn't know who her teacher was, but she should have taught her to be a better dancer and a better sport!

Another time, one of my own students had a melt-down when she didn't place in the finals of a contest. She screamed, "OH NO!" and ran out of the room crying. I was mortified. Then she went around confronting the judges and asking them why she didn't place. They were mortified. This was a woman who wanted to make a career of dance. Her lack of composure and confrontation were the beginning of her career demise.

People who compete only to win shouldn't be competing. Dancers who dance from their ego instead of their heart shouldn't be competing either. They are missing out on a learning opportunity and missing the point completely.

Belly dancing gave me the courage to overcome many of my fears, the fear of driving, the fear of phones, the fear of being on a stage and the fear of public speaking. It gave me the courage to step out into the world and have a life full of adventure, the courage to make friends and travel.

Belly dancing also gave me pride in myself as a person. It has saved my life in many ways, literally kept me alive during deep depressions and gave me a life that is fulfilling and filled full. And my confidence started when I forced myself to step onto the stage at my very first competition. I was greatly rewarded for taking that risk, rewarded with dance opportunities and lifetime friendships.

16 CHALLENGES AND TROUPES

When I first started writing this book, I just wanted to write about all the positive things the dance has given me. I wanted to inspire others by my own experience and encourage others to use the dance as a tool to heal. But, as I got further into it, I realized that by leaving out the hard experiences, I was being less than honest.

There is a dark and light side to everything in life, and thus the balance is maintained.

Fortunately, for me, the light and beauty of the dance far outweigh the darkness, but in all honesty, I need to include the darkness in my healing journey. For, to find healing, I also had to wrestle with the pain of lost sisters and do it with grace and discretion.

I always say that belly dancing is a sisterhood, and that we are like a family. For most of us this is true, but we sometimes forget that families don't always get along. My own life is a testament to that since my parents and three sisters disowned me so many years ago.

Just like biological sisters, belly dance sisters sometimes bicker, sometimes hurt each other's feelings and sometimes suffer from jealousy. It's how we handle our wounds that make a difference.

With every challenge, there comes a lesson, and we can choose whether or not to accept the lesson. I also perceive the people who challenge me as my teachers, and while the lesson may be hard at the time, such as my husband falling in love with a troupe member, I'm always grateful for it later.

There are politics in everything, no matter how hard we try to avoid it.

I handle belly dance politics by what I call "being Switzerland." I don't take sides. I can't tell you how many times I've had both sides of a feuding couple of friends confide in me. Neither dancer knows the other has told me her side of the story. Sometimes it can be uncomfortable, but usually I am just internally amused.

When dancers aren't getting along and confide or vent to me, I try to help them 'get over it.' Often I can see that it has just been a simple misunderstanding, or gossip mongers in overdrive. I try to be a wise counsel suggesting that there may have been a misunderstanding and encouraging them to talk to the other person. Or, I can be pretty blunt and tell them that they shouldn't listen to gossip.

My first dance partner/sister/friend was a piece of work. I credit her with teaching me how to hug and I will always be grateful to her for that one thing. It might not seem like much to some of you, but to me, a person who didn't like to touch or be touched, it was a monumental gift. She would give me a hug, and ask me to hug her back. I thought I was, but she taught me that I was just going through the motions, not really giving.

The flip side to this story was that she was also superficial and jealous. Together, we put on my first event, inviting a dancer from Seattle to come teach a workshop and dance in a show. We rented the senior center, and it was a huge success. We did a couple of more shows after that. While we came up with the plans together, I ended up doing most of the leg work which was no problem for me. It became a problem when the newspaper wrote an article about our efforts and mentioned my name once more then her name was mentioned. She blew up saying that I got all of the glory.

Men flocked around this women like flies to honey, but one night a man winked and waved at me when we were at a dance gig and she flipped out with jealousy. It was a complete shock to me that she would be jealous of me. She was petite, and I was big. She was gorgeous, and I was just pretty. She was a wonderful dancer, and got all the attention when we performed with people cheering while she danced and politely clapping after I performed. So, how could she possibly be jealous of me?

It wasn't long before she was divorced, and she was very depressed. I spent a lot of time with her, a lot of hand holding and supporting her through her painful process. A year later, I was going through a divorce and when I turned to her for support, these were her actual words: "You are depressed and a big downer. I don't want to be around you right now." I was bereft, betrayed and totally alone. Apparently our relationship was one-directional giving. I gave, and she took. I didn't learn the lesson this time.

My next big challenge came when I had my son. My pregnancy was difficult, and my son was a needy baby. I didn't sleep for more than two hours a day for months. I started my classes when Logan was two weeks old, desperate to gain back some sense of normalcy in my life. I also tried to have troupe practice again. But, one of my best friends, and best dancers didn't show up for practice three weeks in a row. She had never missed practice before, was my most dedicated dancer, and I didn't know what was going on. When I asked her about it, she had excuses like Dr. appointments.

As it turns out, she had joined another dancer's troupe, someone else I thought of as a close friend. Instead of just telling me and being honest about it, I found out when I first saw them dancing together. Neither one of them told me what was literally going on behind my back.

At the time I was devastated, feeling like I had been kicked in the gut and stabbed in the back. My heart was truly broken. I was also suffering from postpartum depression, so it made things seem so much worse. It would have been so much better if they'd been up front with me and told me what was going on. Finding out the way I did was a very cruel blow.

I had held both of these dancer's hands during family tragedies and illness, but when I needed support, it wasn't there. Again, I gave and gave never thinking that when I had a need, they wouldn't be there for me. But, they weren't, and there was that lesson again.

This time, with the help of a friend, I understood the lesson. I was good at giving, but not so skilled at receiving, which created friendships/relationships that were out of balance. With her help and the help of other friends on a spiritual path, I learned to receive. I remember when Logan was almost a year old, they threw me a surprise birthday party, telling me that they could see I was all given out and needed something back. It was a gift of love that I will always cherish.

For awhile, I stayed pretty isolated from the dance community at large. I no longer did troupe dancing, instead doing duets with my beautiful daughter and relishing every moment. Most of my students were now transient, finding out about me when they came to the Ken Keyes College, a new age type school in the town I lived in. These students were from all over the world, and I had a great time meeting people and having fun teaching them briefly, but beautifully the art of belly dance until they left to return to their country taking a new skill home with them.

When my son was five, I fell in love and moved to a new town, Sutherlin, Oregon. There I started a new family of dance sisters. My mother-in-law, was a teacher in the area but taught in the privacy of her home without advertising. So, I was the first in many years to 'publicly' teach belly dancing in the area.

Time after time, I heard, "I've wanted to take belly dancing for years, and you are the first teacher I've found." I taught for several years through the local community college, and again many students were transient and left when they left for the university. But, several local women have stayed with me for years.

It wasn't long before I formed another troupe this time called Mystical Mirage by picking five of my best students. For awhile, we had a great time. A husband of one dancer and the son of another began learning to drum, so we had live music in our group which was a first for me. When things began to really get good, a jealousy issue popped up. No matter what I said, or how I tried to handle it, things only got worse until the troupe broke up. At one point, the husband drummer even threatened to kill one of the other dancers. As much as I was disappointed losing the troupe, I was even more relieved to be free of the drama.

For me, this was a lesson about jealousy. It was something I was unfamiliar with. What I learned about myself is that I wasn't a jealous person, that I was happy for other people when they succeeded, etc. It made me feel better about myself.

I thought about the term, 'green with envy,' and decided the green came from pus. Envy and jealousy are like a festering sore that breaks open and begins to pus. When untreated, it turns into gangrene and is followed by death. In this case, it was death of my troupe.

I took a short break from troupe dancing and then in the year 2000, I started another troupe called, Mystical Oasis Dance Co. I posted a flyer on my studio door saying that anyone who was interested could join.

The troupe became a mix of my students and my student's students, and after a couple of years of watching us have a great time, one of my former students asked if she could join the troupe. Of course, I welcomed her with open arms.

Almost immediately, a clique started forming. I take great pride in the fact that my troupe is made up of women of all shapes, sizes and abilities. I also make sure our costuming is flattering to everyone, no matter their figure. But this new clique became dissatisfied, and decided that troupe wasn't challenging enough. And, by the way, why did they have to wear the same costuming as the 'fat' girls?

I took them aside individually and talked to them about the importance of the group, how some moves were too advanced for all the dancers and how it was important to wear costuming that was flattering for everyone. I choreographed a routine that had the more advanced dancers doing more advanced moves hoping to fill everyone's needs.

We worked hard towards dancing in a big event in Portland. As the date got closer, the tension built as dancers sniped among themselves. I kept hoping that people would get over their individual 'diva' attitudes, leave their egos at the door and have fun. No matter how hard I talked, how loving and accepting I tried to be, nothing worked.

By the time the big performance arrived, I was a basket case. I couldn't wait to get it over with. It was a personal disaster. My whole life was about love, and this group of women was not acting very loving. What was going on?

This time I tried a new tactic. The practice after the big performance, I sat everyone down in a circle. I started by reading a poem about the sisterhood of the dance. Next, I said that I wanted this time to be a time of healing. I brought out a Native American talking stick and said that we would pass it from person to person and while the person who held the stick talked, the rest of us would listen without interrupting. I said that this wasn't a time to point fingers or place blame, and that I wanted each person to take the stick and state how they could personally make troupe practice a more positive experience, and one thing they wanted out of troupe.

Unfortunately, the first person to accept the stick took the opportunity to go into full attack mode. Now keep in mind that just three days before, this same person sent me a beautiful thank you note telling me what a wonderful friend I was, how much I had helped her and what a blessing it was to have me in her life. That night, she all but called me Hitler, went on for over 20 minutes attacking my teaching methods, my integrity, the dance, other dancers, etc. The next person took her lead. Attack and blame aimed mostly at me. Then there was Jasel, coming to the defense.

I'll never forget what she said. "This is Mezdulene's troupe and Mezdulene's studio. She graciously invited you to be here and if you don't like it, you can leave." She said some other good stuff, standing up for me, a true friend trying to redirect the flow of negativity.

Then there was Masahti, another true friend who said how much she cared about me and the troupe and then offered to leave the troupe if we felt that would be helpful to the common good.

I didn't have the talking stick, but inside I was yelling, "You're not the problem!"

So, to make a really long story shorter, the 'skinny' clique left the troupe to start their own thing. We went from 11 weak to 5 strong, and it was like a huge weight was lifted off of us. The poison was expelled and troupe became fun again.

The grandiose plans of the defectors came to naught, and most of them quit dancing all together. It's sad that so much talent was overtaken by ego and the joy of dance lost.

The breakup occurred on a Monday, and that Friday I had an emergency appendectomy. It felt like all of their venom caused my appendix to fill up with toxins and become inflamed and burst. As they wheeled me towards surgery, we passed the waiting area where I was touched to see a large group of my students waiting.

After surgery, several of my friends and students came and gave me Reiki. I was very ill, and the doctor said I would need to be there for at least 2-3 nights. Instead, I was able to go home in less than 24 hours due to the love and healing energy of my friends. It was amazing and wonderful!

A few weeks later, I printed an article in 'Jareeda' about my painful experience with troupe and gave some suggestions on positive ways to leave a troupe. I got a ton of feedback on that article from other troupe directors all saying they were glad they weren't the only ones, or thanking me for writing the articles or thanking me for the suggestions I gave in the article.

The most interesting letter I received was from the dance guild I belonged to saying that my article violated their standards and they threatened to kick me out because I bad mouthed another guild member. I wrote them back and pointed out that the article had no names and that the person who created the drama I wrote about was not a guild member and that they had made a wrong assumption. I also said I was not bad mouthing but relating a factual incident and possible healthier solutions and that many other dancers had found my article helpful. They changed their tune.

Since then we have been wary of whom we allow into our troupe, and even so, we've still been burned. Each time the tension gradually builds and then releases when the person leaves. We work hard to create an outstanding routine, sew our fingers to the bones making a new costume and someone decides to leave, usually in a hurtful way which I don't understand. I had one student leave because she felt overwhelmed, felt like she had bit off more then she could handle and needed more family time. There were no pointing fingers, no angry words, just integrity and taking responsibility for her own issues. Kudos! She should teach seminars on diplomacy!

Over the years I've seen women leave the dance because of hurt feelings, because so and so said this or so and so did that. I've seen a few of them return to the dance and regret leaving, regret the lost years. People come and go, but the dance and music are always there for us. How sad when people turn away from something that brings joy because of petty differences.

As I said earlier, there are times when sisters don't get along, but it's our choice how we treat each other. We can place blame or we can accept responsibility. I'm not perfect, but I make it a policy not to say anything behind your back that I wouldn't say to your face. And, I want the dance to be an enriching and fun experience for everyone.

Stick with me and you will go places, baby!!

Now that I've written about the challenges of our sisterhood, I'd like to end this chapter on an up note.

I want to say that Mystical Oasis Dance Company has been such a huge blessing in my life. There is something about dancing with a group of women that nourishes me in a way that nothing else can ever come close to. When I dance as a soloist, I often reach a state of bliss where I feel a strong spiritual connection. I actually feel love pouring through me, into my heart and out my arms, into my hands and then pouring out to the audience. It is amazing and fulfilling. When I dance in a group, I feel a connection to my sister dancers, a different kind of bliss.

Mystical Oasis Dance Company
Front: Azuul Khayal Back L to R: Jasel, Masahti, Mezdulene

My troupe is exactly what I have always wanted. They are so much more than dance-mates; they are my sisters, sisters of the heart instead of the body. We have all been there for each other through multiple life challenges from births to deaths and everything in between.

We choreograph, make costumes, travel and perform, but we also support each other emotionally. Sometimes our practices become group therapy, sometimes individual therapy. For me, the past few years have tested me with divorce and so much loss, stressful to say the least. My troupe-mates have been an ongoing support, and troupe practice has been my sanctuary.

We do leave our everyday lives at the door, but sometimes it's hard to leave our pain and being together, talking and dancing is the greatest healing balm in the world. We may enter the studio suffering, but we leave it lifted up by our sisters, encouraged, loved and supported. As we go back into our daily grinds, we carry with us the joy we shared in troupe, and we look forward to our next time together, our next dance, our next costume, our next adventure in life!

I asked two of my core troupe members to write about their troupe experiences, and I can't say it any better.

Jasel:
What is a Troupe?

Troupe is love and acceptance
a safe place to be
where laughter rings loudly
where tears can flow free

Troupe means commitment
not just to each other
but commitment to the dance
that we create together

Troupe is where hugs abound
when I am needy or happy
screaming in anger or feeling lost
or celebrating a new love found

Troupe creates expectations
to be so very very much more
to open your soul, to create, to dance
to spread your wings and soar

Troupe is a sacred space
where you can fall apart
and rebuild, a place to hide safely
the place I needed for healing to start

Troupe was my salvation not so very long ago
I survived this trial of my life because
it helped keep despair and insanity from taking hold
kept my head held high not hung low

Troupe holds my sisters smiles
their unconditional love for me
these beautiful women who live in my heart
whose love and joy set my soul free

Troupe to Jasel is dancing
dancing with light and love
dancing with joy and passion
dancing with laughter and fun

Join a troupe today
and you will soon see
you can also feel this way
"My Troupe completes me."

Masahti *"My life as a troupie"*

Ten years ago, I started my life as a performance dancer. I had been taking dance classes for just over a year; I had absolutely no intention ever of dancing as a soloist, but Mezdulene, my teacher, was beginning a new troupe, and I thought it would be fun to dance with the group. I had no idea how dancing and the relationships I began with that fateful decision would change my life.

Our original troupe was seven women. The youngest was 16, the oldest was something older than 60 (she would never tell her age, but did admit to having danced once with Donald Conner, who acted in Singing in the Rain.) We were sized extra small to extra large, both in height and in girth, and were from all walks of life. The only thing we had in common was a love of dance. Once a week we would get together and just dance. It was a transforming experience. Our first dances were quite simple, but we all discovered something magical when we danced together. The art of all working together, on "the same wavelength" to create art together, is one that is impossible to describe. More, I have found a sisterhood and a sense of self through troupe that I didn't know I was lacking.

My husband and I had been married for two years when we decided to try to have a baby. We had been trying for about nine months when I found out I was pregnant. I was ecstatic. I told everyone. That night, I began to bleed, and learned first-hand the grief and sense of failure that comes from miscarriage. I later learned that an estimated 25 to 50% of all pregnancies end in miscarriage; the knowledge didn't help ease the pain. What did help was the love and support from my sisters in troupe, as well as the routine of dance. I had to fake the joy our dances felt, and with time, I began to feel the joy again, too.

When my daughter was born almost exactly one year after I lost the first baby, my sisters were just as supportive. They allowed for a leave of absence when I couldn't dance due to pregnancy complications, and welcomed both me and baby Elizabeth into the troupe for as long as I was unwilling to put her down even long enough to dance. I had to go back to work when Elizabeth was three months old, and Jasel became a surrogate "auntie" and watched my baby, even bringing her to me at work so that we could nurse over my lunch hour.

This is not to say that everything has always been positive. Even the best of sisters sometimes fight. At various times, we have argued, spat insults at each other, said hateful things, and generally been poorly behaved. Some of these arguments have led to women leaving troupe, sometimes en mass. However, even in the most hateful times, I've never felt the desire to leave. I've learned that sisters may fight, but troupe lives on, and the love and support I feel from the group never ends.

Troupe has given me personal support, but they also have supported me in my growth as a dancer. Because of troupe, I gained the confidence to try soloing. I have learned to adjust on stage, improvise when necessary, and not to stick my tongue out when I mess up. I have learned to NOT improvise costume pieces out of raw material. [belts should NEVER be replaced with a length of raw chiffon] I have learned to choreograph a dance for multiple people and have learned to accept that my vision is not necessarily everyone's vision. I have learned to be a piece of the whole and to redefine the whole when someone is ill or injured.

The original Mystical Oasis Dance Company has changed in the ten years since it was formed. It grew from seven to eleven women, imploded, shrank as low as three, and has steadied out now at four members. These women are as close to me now as my own sisters. My troupe members grieved with me when I miscarried my first baby, rejoiced with me when both my children were born, were accepting when I danced with my babies even while dancing with the troupe, put up with my whining about how crazy my life is, and come support my drama students in their plays. With the support and reliance of my troupe, I have continued to grow as a dancer, rather than stagnate and eventually drop out, as seems to happen to so many. Jasel, Mezdulene, and Zivah are all women with whom, in the normal course of my life, I would have no contact. Through the magic of the "Mystical Oasis Dance Divas," they have become the sisters of my heart.

17 MEZDULENE

Mezdulene is not my birth name.

I know, you're just shocked, aren't you? Not! However, Mezdulene is my 'real' name, and many years ago, it also became my legal name.

Over thirty years ago, when I was just a young belly dancer, I met a friend of my friend's little sister. We had gone out dancing, and in these situations I was usually the odd woman out and just sat and watched. But, this time was very different.

I don't remember his name, and our connection was very brief, but as it turns out, deep. For this purpose, I'll call him, Amir.

Amir and I began to talk, and as it turns out, we were both dance teachers. He taught American swing dance in Saudi Arabia, and I taught Middle Eastern dance in America. We laughed together at the irony, and then he asked me to dance.

I told him that I didn't know how to swing dance, had never done it and that I only knew how to belly dance. He gently insisted, and I finally gave in. I am very glad I did, because it's an experience I've always carried with me.

Out on the dance floor, he told me to just relax and let him do all the work, and somehow I was actually able to do it. I just let go, and I was swung around here and there, spun around, swung out and in and it was just amazing! What a fun experience it was to dance with a man, and ever since then I have wanted to learn swing dancing or ballroom dancing, but it hasn't happened.

After we danced, we talked more, and somehow the subject of wanting a Middle Eastern stage name came up. He told me three names that he thought would fit me, and I chose Mezdulene.

He and his friends left, and I never saw him again, but I have been Mezdulene ever since that night so long ago.

To this day, I've never met another Mezdulene, and for a time I began to wonder if it was even a real name. Then one day, a few years ago, a food vendor at a belly dance festival in Seattle said, "Mezdulene is a good name and that it meant she who brings joy into the space or room."

I asked him why I never hear of anyone with my name and he told me it was because it's an old name like, Matilda or Gertrude is in our country and that no one uses the name anymore.

So, mystery solved!

In the year 2000, I decided to legally change my name. It wasn't something I did on a whim, but something I had given a great amount of thought to. It wasn't because I disliked my birth name; it was about celebrating me, the person that I had become.

Before I became a belly dancer, I was a victim. My life had been about abuse, rejection, betrayal and so much emotional pain. With the help of the dance, I re-created myself. I got in touch with my femininity. I got therapy. I worked hard on healing, read self-help books and completely changed myself from the inside out.

I was no longer a victim; I was a strong woman and a leader.

By letting go of my old name, I was letting go of the victim I had been. By embracing my new name, I was embracing the new me.

It was a deeply personal transition, and yet at the same time, a public one.

It didn't seem like that big of a deal since most people only knew me by the name Mezdulene. I was done with my old name. It belonged to the abused child, betrayed wife, and disowned daughter.

At first Mezdulene was like a role I slipped into. It was a stage name, and as Mezdulene, I was a dancer. I could dance in front of hundreds of people with grace and composure. I was a teacher, a public speaker, and later a magazine publisher. As Mezdulene, I felt strong and confident. My innate shyness slipped away along with the myriad of fears that had held me back my entire life.

As the years passed, Mezdulene became more and more me and less and less a role until one day I realized 'I am Mezdulene.' I was a self-created person, a person who had worked hard to overcome the abuse and rejections of her earlier life, a person who was no longer shy and depressed, but friendly and motivated. It was fine when I first started dancing to take on the persona of 'Mezdulene' to overcome my shyness and stage fright, but I was no longer that person, I was the same me on stage that I was off stage. I liked who I had become, and changing my name was a way to validate myself and honor what I had overcome and what I had accomplished.

Just for fun, one day I went on-line and Googled myself. There were thousands of hits all referring to me. Cool! My old name? No hits referring to me but lots referring to other people with that same name. Any other Mezdulene's in the world? Maybe not. I love my name!

I have had several friends change their names over the years. One friend named Robin changed her name to River, Carla wanted to be Freddie, a friend called Patty wanted to be called Patricia, and the list goes on. I didn't think anything about it; while it took some time to remember to call them by their new name, it wasn't a big deal. It's what they wanted, so I called them by their new name.

Imagine my surprise when I got a bunch of negativity about my name change. It wasn't just surprising, it was also hurtful.

At first I was very relaxed about the whole thing and told people they could call me by either name. I realize it's a change, and some people don't like change, but it quickly became a sore point. I began to see that people, who cared about my feelings, had no problem with calling me, Mezdulene or Mez for short. However, people who cared only about their own feelings refused. They even acted angry that I would dare impose on them in such a way. "That's not your name! I'll never call you that!"

Really?

My husband refused to call me Mezdulene or Mez because "that's not who he married." (That was interesting because I thought he married me, not my name.) He didn't understand why I chose to make the name, Mezdulene my legal name. Well, I didn't understand some things about him, but I accepted them because I loved him.

And then there was my sister-in-law and mother-in-law who said they wouldn't call me Mezdulene because they've always known me by my other name, my real name.

Really?

Well, guess what? The truth is that they met me at a dance event. I was only called Mezdulene at dance events, so they didn't find out my other name until later. They have always known me as Mezdulene. It wasn't some new name plucked out of the universe during a mid-life crisis, such as Sage Dreamer or Moon Drummer. It had been my name for over 20 years, and is the name that most people in the world called me. And, the name they insisted was my real name was really a nickname, not my birth name. So what the heck was going on here?

One night, at a family dinner, I became a point of ridicule when I introduced myself to someone as Mezdulene. Family members made fun of me and belittled me and said things like they liked the old me but not the new me. I told them that changing my name wasn't about them, that it was about me, a decision I made for my highest good, and then I got up and left before I burst into tears. I was devastated.

I received an email from one of them telling me how they liked the old me but didn't like Mezdulene, because Mezdulene hurt her feelings. I wrote back and asked her why it was okay for her to ridicule me and hurt my feelings, but not okay for me to stand up for myself.

How did legalizing a name I'd been called since long before they knew me, change me? Why were the very people I thought would understand, threatened and angry? What was the big deal?

I reached the point where I no longer felt relaxed about it. I honor the personal choices of my loved ones, and it never even occurred to me that they wouldn't honor mine. The very people I thought would be supportive were the ones who were least supportive. I expected this to be an interesting process, but I didn't expect it to be a painful one.

I knew it would take people time to adjust, but to go into attack mode?

My husband refused to call me Mezdulene and continued to introduce me to new friends by my old name. I finally lost my temper, and it wasn't pretty. I was angry, hurt, crying and yelling all at the same time.

I told him that changing my name was important to me, and that he had helped me become strong enough to be myself in the world, and now he didn't care enough about me to call me by my real name. It wasn't like something I did on a whim or a name I grabbed out of the air, it was the name most people in the world knew me by and had known me by for over twenty years. And, if it was important to me, then as my husband, it should be important to him.

After I claimed my power, he finally, grudgingly started calling me Mez but never Mezdulene. At the time, I was hurt, but I wasn't ready to look at the deeper issues in our marriage.

Changing my name was my own personal choice and a tangible way of claiming the positive in my life, a statement of personal empowerment. It has also turned out to be a great lesson to me in other ways and was a major step towards accepting the Divine Feminine.

What has belly dance given you?

What choices have you made in your own life to claim the positive?

What lessons have you learned?

Does it make you uncomfortable when your loved ones choose to heal or change their lives for the better?

If so, why do you think you feel uncomfortable?

What personal changes do you want to make?

What keeps you from making them?

What is your heart's desire? Stand up for yourself. You are the only one who knows your own heart and mind, the only one who can make the changes you need for healing. Please don't let anything or anyone hold you back from your dreams.

18 ADVENTURE

I love adventure! I love traveling to new places and meeting new people. I am fascinated by other cultures and other religions.

As a child living on the reservation, I was fascinated by the culture and traditions of the Apaches. Whenever I could, I'd sneak out and go to a ceremony or celebration either watching from afar or being in the middle of the action and dancing the friendship dance. As a teenager, I realized that my culture didn't have tradition, that I didn't know my own heritage, and I was envious of my friends who knew stories and songs that had been passed down through generations. I was captivated by the medicine men and medicine women, who helped heal people and the witches who could be paid to put a curse on people.

So, I guess it's not a stretch that I became enamored by a dance from the Middle East. Almost from the beginning belly dance has been an avenue to adventure, and I'd like to share some of them.

One of my first adventures was dancing in the show I mentioned in Seattle with George Abdo, live. I already wrote about the thrill of dancing while a singing legend, crooned. But, what I didn't mention was meeting John Compton.

John was the first male belly dancer I ever laid eyes on. He was gorgeous with piercing blue eyes and a stage presence unlike any other. My partner and I danced in the first half of the show and we were in the front row for the second half when John danced. It was a huge audience of around 450 people, and I swear every woman there was on her feet and screaming except for us because we wanted to be cool. But, on the inside, we were both screaming too!

He balanced a huge tray on his head, and on the tray were a brass pitcher and some cups. His dance was masculine and exciting, but his mood shifts kept us intrigued. He would go from serious and dramatic to winking and wiggling his eyebrows. What an amazing entertainer.

Another dancer I met that night was Phaedra. She was like a queen on the stage. She and John did a duet that was so masterful and so emotively potent; I have never seen anything that compared to it. Little did I know that in my second year of dancing I would experience a highlight unlike any I would ever again witness.

In the dressing room, I told Phaedra I loved her head piece. She said, "Really? I was worried it might be too big. Do you think I should wear it this way, or this way?"

She was asking me? This gorgeous Goddess was asking me, a baby belly dancer my opinion? Oh my gosh, I never forgot that moment when I realized that she, too was nervous, no different than me.

Rakkasah is held in Richmond, California, not far from San Francisco, and it's the largest belly dance festival in the world. I first went there with my friend Halima and one of her friends, Pat. It's an amazing event held in a huge room with a huge stage. There are over a hundred vendors there selling everything imaginable from around the world. And, there is non-stop dancing for over 30 hours during the weekend. For the first-time attendee, it can be overwhelming, a sensory overload.

This first year, we decided to go to the store for something after the festival was over at 11 p.m. We got lost on the way back to our motel and stopped at a convenience store to ask for directions. The young lady behind the counter said she would give us directions only if we made her a promise. We gave each other puzzled looks and asked her what she wanted us to promise. She said that where we were staying was okay, but between here and there was dangerous. She wanted us to promise that if anything happened, we wouldn't stop and that even if we had a flat tire to keep driving on the rim until we got back to our motel. We promised, got our directions and an adrenaline rush all at the same time. We made it back safely only to find that some people's rooms and cars had been broken into, not such a safe motel after all. That was enough excitement for us, and we decided to find a new place to stay.

One year I went to a big festival in Los Angeles to vend, *Jareeda*

138

Magazine. I flew in and met up with my pal, Gaylene and we shared a motel room.

Los Angeles isn't my favorite place. I'm definitely a country girl, and while I think it's awesome that there is so much diversity and opportunity in that city, I don't like chewing my air. The pollution is intense, and driving down the freeway was like a scene from the futuristic movie with Kurt Russell called 'Escape from L.A.' There was graffiti everywhere, and there was razor wire along all the overpasses and around the power poles and street lights.

My booth was outdoors, and it was at least 100 degrees. I also don't do heat well, so there I was in the bathroom pulling my shirt off, soaking it in the sink and putting it back on while people gave me strange looks.

I was disappointed that the stage was indoors and I didn't get to see even one performance, and ever since then I've learned to ask what the stage and vending set-up is. I don't go just to make money. I have to pay for my habit, but the real point of going to these events is to see the dancing!

So, after an unusual weekend, I was at the airport and the next thing I know, it's shut down. There was a bomb threat. I felt like I was in an alien land. So, there I was sitting outside reading and waiting for them to find the bomb. I looked up and watched the planes flying over that couldn't land, and was amazed to see what looked like a freeway in the sky. I have never seen so many planes flying so close together in my life. First, 'Escape From L.A. and now 'The Jetsons!'

Well, I finally made it home safe and sound, and I haven't been back. I have several friends who live and dance down there, but I like bringing them to me or seeing them at other events.

Remember when I said that early on in my dance life I had to drive over 400 miles to find a workshop? Well, drive to San Francisco we did! Me, my dance partner and student, Ameena drove down for a workshop and show with some big names of the business. The event was sponsored by the original owner of *'Habibi'* a former dance publication, and we had high expectations. The highlights of that weekend were Ameena sleeping in her clothes in case the motel caught fire so she didn't have to run outside in her nightie, and the big name belly dancers being pretty awful. The workshops were good, but the show was a big lesson for us. We put on better shows, in our little isolated town, and we learned that being a big name didn't mean you were a good dancer. We found out that we were better than we realized, and Ameena stopped trying so hard to be perfect and started just dancing to have fun and went on to become an amazing dancer.

There are always benefits to traveling out of town to other events, but the benefits aren't always what we might expect.

My trip with Halima to the Salt Lake City Belly Dance Festival was filled with adventure. There were the car problems I mentioned and becoming the new owner of *Jareeda*. But, there was also the part where we got lost and stopped to ask for directions. It was a tiny town that consisted of a diner, convenience store and gas station in one building and a motel consisting of some old trailers, plus a real estate sign saying, 'Town For Sale.'

When we went in to ask for directions, it was a pretty creepy place where all eyes turned to look at us. No one could give us a straight answer, and Halima gave me a gentle nudge, a look and said quietly, "Let's get out of here."

We quickly jumped in the truck and started to drive away while she commented that they looked like cannibals and reminded her of the movie, 'The Hills Have Eyes.' Now, those of us who know Halima, know she likes her horror movies, and you might think she was being melodramatic, but I was there, and they did look at us like they were planning their next meal! Yikes!

A few years ago, the sponsor of Rakkasah started 'Rakkasah East,' held in New Jersey. My ex-husband and I flew there, and we had the most amazing time. I'd never been to the east coast and neither had he. The festival was great, much smaller than the west coast event, but still wonderful. However, the best part about this adventure was going to New York City.

Now, let me say I had never in my life had any desire to go to NYC. Remember, I'm a country girl all the way. I love nature and the great outdoors, so the thought of going to a giant city was not an appealing one.

BUT! That all changed. I was lured there by a belly dance event, and had so much fun, I went back again.

All my life, I've heard how dangerous NYC was and told not to wear nice jewelry so you don't get mugged, etc. I also heard that people there were very self-involved and unfriendly.

Well, let me tell you! That was not my experience of New York at all. Maybe if I'd gone when I was still a victim and living in fear things might have been different, but I had the absolute best time.

First we rode a train to the city, and then we went on a subway. This was a first for both of us. We ended up at Grand Central Station, and we went to Little Italy, and then while wandering the streets we came to a Buddhist temple.

On our first subway ride, we were sitting there minding our own business and this group of black men said "Excuse me. Please give us your attention!" They were holding open a brown paper bag and my first thought was we were going to be robbed just like I'd been warned and just like in the movies. They were going to pass the bag around and make us put our valuables in it.

My bad! The reality? They started singing a cappella, and the bag was for tips. They were pretty amazing, and a real treat.

While in New York, we went to the top of the Empire State Building, and the most amazing thing about that was how small the island looked. There are millions of people in a little tiny space! In the west, the cities spread out, but there they just go up!

I wanted to go to the Egyptian art show, but it was closed so we ended up at the natural history museum. It would have taken days to see it all, but we saw the rock and gem section and some huge specimens. And, we saw 'Lucy' the 3.2 million year old skeleton of an ancestor of humans.

We also went to St. Peter's Cathedral, and I was absolutely entranced. I have never seen anything man-made that is so beautiful. All of the ornamentation carved in stone was just incredible. I could have stayed in there for hours, and in fact did stay for mass, but I don't remember a thing except looking up, down and all around. The cathedral is massive, and the fact that it was all carved by hand is mind-blowing.

When we came out of the cathedral, we were approached by a big blonde guy with a bicycle rickshaw who offered to give us a ride. We were starving so asked him to take us to a good place to eat. It was an exciting ride as he dashed in and out of traffic during rush hour, and he took us to a Scottish pub. It was delightful. I had my first Haggis and drank my first Scottish ale. Yum!

It was a romantic and memorable evening to be sure!

We did lots more, but those were the highlights. Oh, and the unfriendly people? Balderdash!

I didn't meet one rude person in NYC, not even one. We rarely knew where we were going and even when we did have a destination, we didn't have a clue how to get there, so I was always asking directions of perfect strangers, and they were always very gracious.

I think it helped that I'd put it this way: "Excuse me. I'm from a town with one street light, and I'm lost. Can you tell me how to get to.....?" I think they took pity on me when they heard the one street light story which happened to be a true story. Now our town has three streetlights!

My friend, Kashani, invited me to go with her to Maine where she had some family business to attend to. It was going to be a three week trip, and I looked up belly dancers on-line and sent emails asking if anyone would like me to teach a class. I ended up with three workshops in Boston and Maine, and I had such a great time.

It's very different on the east coast compared to the west coast. For instance, the buildings are a lot older and don't have elevators. And, the studios I taught at were all on the top floor where space was more affordable. That meant, schlepping my stuff up several flights of stairs.

I met some awesome dancers during my trip with Kashani, and we had a lot of fun together. She showed me the sights which included old churches and old cemeteries. I love old cemeteries, the history of them, the beautiful headstones, and the peaceful atmosphere. I noticed that each one had doors into the hillside, and I asked her what they were. She told me they were crypts where bodies were stored during the winter because the ground was too frozen to dig, and they had to wait until spring to be buried. That's something you never see that here in the west!

We also drove across a suspension bridge which was just plain, freaky, and we hiked into a famous waterfall. The trail to the waterfall was really long, and we were getting tired and wondered how much further it was to our destination. We passed some people coming back from that direction, and we asked them if it was worth it to keep going. They assured us it was, that we were just going to love the gorgeous waterfall; it was so wonderful and amazing. Those weren't their exact words, but you get the gist of it. We kept hiking, and hiking, and we finally heard running water. It wasn't very loud, but it was running water. The fact is, it never got very loud, and when we got to the end of the trail, we just burst out laughing, that kind of hysterical laughter when you're really, really tired. Anyway, some people were there admiring the waterfall and looking at us like we were lunatics as we laughed. Finally, Kashani caught her breath and told them we hiked all this way expecting a waterfall, and that where we lived this would be considered a small rapid as our waterfalls were hundreds of feet high. Seriously! I had a bigger 'waterfall' in the creek on my property that flooded our driveway years ago. It's all a matter of perspective.

Then, there was the day we went to look for a moose. I was in Maine, and I wanted to see a moose! So we drove out into the country, and sure enough, I got to see a momma moose and her baby trundling down the road. I was very excited! Mission accomplished!

But wait! Now we were lost. We stopped and asked for directions, and a woman told us to follow the road until we got to the tah, and then turn right and it would take us right into town.

I had to ask Kashani for a translation because I had no idea what tah was. As it turns out, it meant tar, what we call asphalt or pavement. In Maine, they also have cahs that drive on the tah, and they eat lobstahs.

What the woman didn't mention was that there were at least twenty forks in the road. Kashani just drove by instinct and took the right or left forks at least a dozen or more times. It started to get dark, and she started to panic. At first she wondered if we were lost, and the next thing I knew she was taking inventory of our food. "Let's see, we have half a bag of nuts, and a bottle of water." I tried to calm her down and said we could always call for help if we needed to, and she freaked. "Don't know you that ¾ of Maine is unexplored wilderness and there is no cell service out here, and we may never be found alive?" The pitch of her voice escalated with each word. Now, I was panicked on the inside but remained calm on the outside. I wasn't panicked because I thought we were lost in the wilderness, I was panicked because my friend was freaking out in the wilderness.

It was about at that point that we saw a car approaching from the opposite direction. I told her to pull into the middle of the road so he would have to stop and not just drive past, and she did, and he stopped.

I jumped out of the car to go ask him for directions. Now, I want you to know that I am a free spirit, and I dress like a free spirit. On this day, I had on a long tie-dyed dress and a multi-colored silk coat that was a patchwork of Indian sari scraps. The reason I mention this is because as I approached his car, the man's eyes got big and he quickly rolled up his window. I yelled, "We're lost." He rolled his window down about an inch and asked me where I was from. I told him I was from the west coast, and he said he didn't know how to tell me to get there. By now, I realized he probably thought I was some kind of 'hippie freako.' I was finally able to explain what we needed and it turned out we were just a mile from the tah.

After we were back in civilization, we laughed as we imagined that guy in the local bar telling his buddies about the weird woman he encountered on his way to the pond.

A few years later, I went back to Maine with another belly dance friend, Sidonia from Boise, Idaho. We had a wonderful time, and I got to see another moose, a lobster hatchery and my favorite part was visiting Little Cranberry Island.

We went on a little cruise to see the wildlife, and my lovely friend let me sit near the side where I could see well. How very thoughtful! As a wave crashed over the side and soaked me, I thought it was thoughtful alright. She thought she wanted a barrier between her and the crashing waves. I gave her a glare, and we laughed our guts out over that one.

We did see a lot of wildlife, and I absolutely loved the island. It's a tiny island with a population of less than 100 people. There are cars there but no licenses, and not much for roads. We walked to the post office, and it was such a quaint village. I loved the energy there, and someday I want to go back and spend some time there writing. You can only reach it by ferry, and I wonder how they grocery shop and how they manage during the winter. What an amazing place!

When I went to Maine with Kashani, I didn't eat lobster until the last day because I didn't like lobster. I had tried it several times but found it to be expensive, dry and tasteless. On our last day there, she insisted I eat lobster, and it was one of the best things I ever put in my mouth. It was heaven in my mouth, and I was so sorry I didn't try it sooner.

Apparently, fresh lobster cooked correctly is food of the gods and goddesses!

So, when I went to Maine with Sidonia, I ate lobster almost every single day. It turns out she is a master when it comes to cooking lobster, and I am a master when it comes to eating it! Fun times for sure!

Recently, I had the pleasure to house sit at a friend's house on the big island of Hawaii. I was there for an entire month! Again, I wrote to dancers on the island. I ended up dancing in a show in Hilo, meeting the local dancers, and I taught a workshop in Kona.

My time on the island was full of magical moments, but the best part was writing this book. What better place to write then a tropical jungle where I could take breaks to see flowing lava actually walking right up to the flow, a green beach with sand made of crushed Peridot, August birthstone and swim with sea turtles.

I've left my best adventure for last, my trip to Egypt.

In 1985, I was in an accident, and my car was totaled. I received whip lash, and wouldn't sign off on any insurance paperwork in case I needed more treatment and promptly went on with my life and forgot about it. After two years, the other person's insurance company called me out of the blue and asked if they gave me $5,000 would I sign their paperwork? Helloooo!!! You bet, I'll sign it.

It never occurred to me to spend that money on anything except for a trip to Egypt.

As long as I could remember, I'd wanted to go to Egypt. I was fascinated by the pyramids and other ruins and the mythology. Then, I became a belly dancer, and my desire to travel there doubled.

I joined up with a tour that was going out of Canada, and I brought my husband, Jack, with me which turned out to be a mixed blessing.

I was told to bring a costume and music because we would be having a dance party on the ship during our Nile cruise. A Nile cruise? Really? I was going to dance on a cruise on the Nile? Woo hoo!!

I'm getting excited just writing about my excitement!

But, first things first; we applied for passports and visas. A happy dance commenced when we received them in the mail.

We met the rest of our group in Vancouver, Canada and flew to Montreal, then NYC where we had a layover. We were told that we were joining another group there who would become part of our tour, a group of people who meditated. So, we met up with them and boarded the giant airplane that was to carry us across the Atlantic. The trip from Vancouver to Egypt took over 24 hours.

On the plane, the dancers were partying, and dancing in the aisles. I was sleeping as much as possible and people teased me, including my husband who was joining right in with the partying. My thought was that I could party anywhere, anytime, but I wanted to be rested when I got to Egypt.

When the plane landed, I felt an immediate sense of peace and it felt like I was home. After landing, we had our first reality check that we were in a third world country. You know how in the U.S. the plane taxis up to the building, and then the tunnel thingie meets the door and you walk out and down the tunnel into the airport?

In Egypt, our plane landed and parked somewhere on the tarmac, we went down the metal stairs onto the tarmac and waited for our luggage to be unloaded. Then, we carried our luggage across the tarmac to the airport and customs. Once we entered the building, it was a real zoo with masses of people.

We had great handlers, and we all made it through customs and onto the bus and to our motel room. Now, remember how everyone had been partying all night? Well, these people, ah-hum, my husband, were getting cranky.

We were told on the bus to our motel that tonight we were going to the temple of Isis, and that it was a temple dedicated to healing. I couldn't wait!!

As it turns out, I was the only one from our dance group who went. All the plane party people were too tired and crashed into bed. So, I left Mr. Cranky Pants and went by myself. Nothing and no one was going to keep me from seeing the temple of Isis.

We had to take a boat out to an island where the temple had been relocated to save it from being flooded when the Aswan dam was built. On the boat, I was with the other group, the one we had joined up with in New York, and I heard them talking about healing. I asked them about it, and they said they did something I'd probably never heard of called, Reiki. Well, as a matter of fact.....

My trip to Egypt turned into even a more amazing adventure. I had the best of both worlds. I did all the dance stuff with the belly dance group and all the sacred stuff with the Reiki group. Who could ask for more? I was truly blessed!

The temple of Isis turned out to be incredible. It was nighttime and they had it all lit up, and it was a great introduction to the wonders of this incredible land.

Each day was a new and unique adventure for me. We saw amazing ancient temples and ruins, and the dancing and music just reached in and grabbed my soul.

It's hard to write about because there was just so much, and my brain is just rushing in every direction remember the sights and sounds and happenings.

I remember that during our flight over there was a point where it occurred to me that I had made such a big deal out of this trip, what if I was disappointed? I had wanted to go since I was a young child, had read every book about Egypt and watched every documentary I could find. What if I got there and it wasn't what I had it imagined to be in my head? What if I freaked out staying in a city of millions of people?

Ha ha ha! It was ten times more amazing then I could ever have imagined and Cairo was like home to me!

One of the first things we did was go to the pyramids since we were staying at the Mena House right near them. We climbed up a ladder in a small, square tunnel, not good for the claustrophobic person, until we came into the upper chamber with a huge sarcophagus. There I could feel a tiny and intense vibration. I was trying to just feel and experience the moment, when an Egyptian man grabbed me, picked me up and tossed me into the sarcophagus. It happened so fast, I couldn't react. He told me I needed to feel the energy there. I guess he had picked up that I was seeing and feeling a different layer then perhaps the average tourist. It was amazing. I can't explain it other than to say, I felt a connection to ancient ones, to the present, the future and to spirit like I was feeling all that was, all that is and all that will be. It sounds like woo woo, and it was woo woo which is why it's hard to put into words.

It was only later, I thought, 'holy cow!' that guy picked me up and tossed me in there like a bag of chips and I'm not a lightweight woman!

There is a lot of speculation about the pyramids, about how they were built, what they were for, their alignment with the heavens, etc. My take on them is that they weren't built by the same people who built the rest of the temples and ruins. I don't know if they were built by aliens or some extinct, advanced civilization, but they weren't built by the same people. Every ruin in Egypt is covered with hieroglyphics and paintings, stories in stone. Inside the pyramid, the walls are completely smooth and a completely different stone then the rest of the ruins. Why would they be so different? They certainly aren't tombs because the tombs of the kings have the stories of their lives all over the walls. I don't believe I was standing in a sarcophagus but that it had a different purpose. What that purpose was, is a complete mystery to me, but it wasn't a coffin.

That day, I also rode a camel. His name was, get ready, Michael Jackson. Jack didn't want to ride a camel. Later on our trip, we had another opportunity to ride and this time he did it. His camel must have smelled his fear because it yanked free from its handler and started heading out into the desert. I can't help but laugh as I write this; the look on his face will live with me forever and his feet kicking in the air, and oh, his squealing. Very funny stuff! Sorry, Jack, but it was really funny and still gives me a laugh whenever I think about it.

Visiting the Valley of the Kings was a remarkable experience. First we went to King Tut's tomb. The tombs are built over the lifetime of the king and because he died at such a young age, his tomb was incomplete. Near the entrance were drawings. As we walked further the drawings were partially painted, and as we got near the burial chamber, they were finished. His chamber was small and covered with beautiful artwork.

As most people probably know, his tomb was found practically intact and spared by tomb robbers. The artifacts are in a museum in Cairo literally piled behind a glass wall. There was so much splendor, jewelry, statues, personal belongings, etc. It is amazing.

What makes it even more amazing is the fact that this was what was in a tiny tomb, one that was built quickly while the body was being embalmed.

Our next stop was Seti's tomb. I can't remember if it was Seti I or Seti II, but it was magnificent. It was absolutely huge! There were immense chambers underground and enormous columns, and every square inch was covered with beautiful artwork. We weren't allowed to take photos, so I have to just cherish my memory of it. And, I can't begin to imagine the artifacts that must have been in there that were totally eradicated by tomb robbers. What a loss, making the discovery of Tut's tomb even more of a piece of fortune!

My very favorite spot was the Temple at Denderah dedicated to Horus' wife, Hathor. It was a beautiful temple and had many different and interesting aspects. The Reiki group invited me to a meditation they had arranged to do in the inner sanctum of the temple, and it ended up being quite the mystical experience where I had what I can only describe as a past life flashback. I could see the temple as it was 2,000 years ago, and I was a priestess and a midwife. I looked down and saw the linen of my dress, felt the air on my face, smelled the odors and it was very, real. Of all the places I visited in Egypt, this was the most profound for me, and someday I'd love to go back there. Here is something I wrote for my creative writing class soon after returning.

Denderah Revisited

The temple Denderah still stands,
a monument to Hathor, the nurturing Goddess.
We explored it with the excitement of children,
from its catacombs to its roof tops
where we could view the panorama of the Sahara
and imagine what might have been.

When it was time to go eat our boxed lunches,
a few of us remained to meditate
in the inner sanctum,
the place of the most holy.
We sat in a circle on the floor,
surrounded by stone of the ancients
carved with stories of old.

When I closed my eyes, I remembered.
The temple filled with light.
Paintings covered the walls in brilliant hues.
The soft fabric of my gown hung lightly from my shoulders
and the life giving Nile sent a breeze
to sift through my hair.

I was young for a priestess,
but I had the touch of Isis.
I could cool fevered brows
and mend injuries with the warmth of my hands.
My thoughts could banish nightmares

and seek out dishonesty.

As I passed into the outer courtyard,
it was bustling with visitors
bringing offerings of thanks.
Their laughing children surrounded me
as I walked to the birthing house.
There I tended to the priestess mothers
and held the babies I would never have
The Great Mother had a different path for me.

I felt a touch on my shoulder,
as I turned, I opened my eyes.
The temple was gray and silent
My head was buzzing with a glowing vibration,
and I brushed the dust of a thousand years from my skirt.
It was time to go eat my box lunch.

I turned to leave the inner sanctum,
and my tour guide fell to the ground.
His body thrashed in unknown pain,
but as I lay my hands on him,
he quieted and opened his eyes.

We toured the magical sights in the early mornings before it got too hot, and rested or shopped in the afternoons.

Having always loved all things Egypt, the shopping was a blast. I was told that they expect you to barter there like they do in Mexico, and being shy I didn't think I could do it. I told Jack it would be up to him. But, when I got there, I became a master at bartering. In fact, it became embarrassing. For instance, at dinner, I'd be wearing a new caftan, and someone else would have one and say, "I got this for only $20! How much did you pay for yours?" I had only paid $5. It wasn't long before I had a trail of other group members following me to learn my methods.

At one point, my shopping fever got me into some trouble. We were on the cruise ship and had stopped to tour a sight at Esna. I had overslept and when I woke up the group had already left the ship. One of the

Egyptian employees, again, picked me up like a bag of chips and swung me over the rail onto land and urged me to catch up with them.

Are Egyptian men like Hercules or something? I have never before or since been picked up by anyone! And, they did it so quickly and easily I had no time to react.

So, I ran up the road and saw the rest of the group up ahead. Walking through this little town was like stepping back in time. The people were wearing galabayahs, there were goats in the street and a donkey pulling a cart. The buildings were made of hardened mud and it was easy to imagine that I had stepped through a time portal. I loved it.

I caught up with my group and then suddenly, there they were! The most beautiful dresses I have ever seen! I asked if we could stop, but they said we were on a tight schedule and had to get back to the ship so we could pass through the next lock in the river. I gave my camera to a friend, asked her to take some photos and stayed behind.

I had to have those dresses for my troupe!

I got the dresses at a great price, but it turned into quite the escapade!

The vendor was a man. He asked me if I would be his friend and I said, yes. He grabbed my boob. I slapped his hand and said that's not what friend means in my country. Then, he grabbed my crotch! I slapped him harder, and repeated what I'd said. So he asked me what friend meant in my country and I told him a friend was someone to talk to. He made a disgusted sound and said that friend was no good in my country!

But I got the dresses! And I got a story to go with them!

I left his booth and walked over to another one that had some beautiful scarves displayed. I asked the woman how much, and she told me. The next thing I knew, the man from the other booth came over and they began a screaming match all in Arabic, and almost instantly I was surrounded by police. Oh my God!

You might imagine my concern, and you might imagine me being a tad scared. Here I was in the boonies of Egypt with a man pulling me by the arm one direction and an old lady pulling me by the other arm the other direction and everyone screaming angrily in a foreign language and the police were there. No one spoke more than a few words of English. Had I done something wrong? Was I going to be carted off to jail?

I was alone without a translator, all because I had to have those darn dresses!

The police calmed everyone down, and I made a hasty exit and headed back to the ship. I think the two shopkeepers were fighting over me, but who knows what it was about.

At one point we were taken to the Khan el Khalili bazaar in Cairo. We were only there for a couple of hours, and I'd like to go back and spend about a couple of weeks just wandering and looking at all the sights. What a remarkable place! There was everything you can imagine being sold there and most of it exotic and beautiful, everything from intricately carved statues to inlaid boxes and perfume bottles. But, of course our focus was on getting belly dance costuming!

I learned early on not to drink anything in the mornings because Egypt doesn't have public restrooms like we do. They did have one at the museum, and one at the Valley of the Kings, but that's all I remember seeing.

So, there we were in the bazaar and I had to go. The shopkeeper spoke fairly good English so I asked him if there was a loo nearby. He said, sure, my nephew will take you. He sent me off with a kid about eight years old, and we went out the back door into an alley. We walked down the alley, and it was like something from one of the Indiana Jones movies. Among the interesting sights, sounds and smells, people were squatted down and cooking over open flames, and kids were playing. We came to a small staircase that clung to the side of a building with no railing and we went up and through a hallway to what turned out to be a private apartment. I can only guess it was the shopkeeper's apartment. The furnishings were very spare, and the bathroom consisted of a sink and an all-purpose hole in the floor with a shower above it.

Who knew that going to the bathroom would become a memorable experience? I'll always remember that bathroom. I know that most countries in the world use holes in the floor or ground, and now that I have arthritic hips, I can't help but wonder how the old people squat and do their business. We are truly spoiled, here in America.

Another thing that happened when we were in the bazaar was it started sprinkling very lightly. Apparently, rain is very rare in Cairo, and people ran for cover like they were being attacked with acid or something. The merchants hurriedly covered their merchandise like it was going to melt. Jack and I are from Oregon where it rains all the time, and we just kept walking along. People were freaking out and trying to get us to come in out of the rain like they were trying to save our lives, again, such a simple thing made interesting.

My first dance experience in Egypt came out of the blue. We were on the cruise ship on the Nile, and the food was a sumptuous feast at every meal. Unfortunately, I didn't get to enjoy the food because I came down with something. As I was leaving the dining room unable to eat lunch, a man called to me and asked if I was a dancer. I told him I was, and he said he wanted me to dance that evening, and I said okay. As far as I knew, it was the night of the dance party, so I didn't think anything of it.

When the time came, I got my costume on, put on a cover-up and took my music down to the lounge area. Soon, live music started and an Egyptian dancer performed. She was gorgeous in a stunning multi-colored sequined dress and very fun to watch. At the end of her performance, the man who had spoken to me earlier came up to me and asked if I had my costume on, and I said yes, under my cover-up. He told me I was next, and I realized I was going to be dancing to this amazing live music on a cruise ship on the Nile in Egypt!!

I didn't feel well, but as soon as I stepped onto the dance floor, I forgot all about that as I was totally lifted up and transported to bliss. I danced for at least 20 minutes, maybe more and never broke a sweat. Unlike what I was used to, Egyptian music was mostly very fast, and until that night, I hadn't really appreciated it very much. Wow! What an experience that was. I had such a wonderful time.

By the time we made it to port at Luxor I was very, very ill, almost unconscious. We had to transfer from the ship to our motel in Luxor. I don't remember much for two days other than wanting to die as I sat in the lobby waiting for a room where I quickly passed out. My next memory was a maid softly stroking my face like an angel of mercy. I missed seeing the sights in Luxor, as I was too ill to go on the tours.

When I was finally able to sit up, I flipped on the television and saw a John Wayne movie dubbed in Arabic. Pretty funny stuff! Once I felt a bit better, I went out and sat on the balcony. My husband was gone, on tour and while I was sitting there the streets filled with military people with machine guns. A roadblock with sand bags was set up at the intersection complete with even bigger guns, and a military truck went down the street announcing something over loudspeakers, of course, in Arabic. I didn't know what was going on. Did world war three just start? Would I ever see my family again? What the heck?

It turns out the king of Zaire was visiting, hence all the hoopla and guns. It was so different then the U.S.

The next night, I was asked to dance at the Old Winter Palace there in Luxor. It turns out the man who had asked me to dance on the ship was the owner of the tour company, and he wanted to see me dance again. Again, I danced to live music, this time with a much bigger band. I still wasn't feeling well and don't remember much about my dance. But, here is what I do remember:

After I performed, I was sitting at our table and a waitperson came and asked me to come with him. He said there was someone who wanted to meet me, and he took me to a different area in back of the restaurant and led me up to, two giant black men in pin-striped suits. They shook my hand, and their hands were so large, my small hand looked like an infant's hand compared to my own hand. They were well over 6 feet tall, and they didn't speak a speck of English. The waitperson didn't speak much English either, but he said that these men were emissaries of the king of Zaire who had sent them to thank me for my beautiful performance.

That was it, and I was then led back to my table.

Can you say, wow?

The next day, I was feeling much better and ventured out into the market place where I was treated like some kind of celebrity. People came up to me and shook my hand, people followed me around, and several told me my dance was very beautiful.

People in my group also poured on the compliments and told me I was much better than the Egyptian dancers. That gave me food for thought because obviously the Egyptian dancers had technique to die for! But, their technique is tiny and precise whereas mine was large and loose, and they stood a lot in one spot whereas I danced all around the room. I think it was my stage presence that made it seem like I was a better dancer; maybe it was my energy which expressed, "I'M DANCING IN EGYPT TO LIVE MUSIC AND I AM IN BLISS, PEOPLE!"

In one place I danced after a troupe of Ghawazee dancers. During their performance, one of the dancers pulled a hankie out of her cleavage and blew her nose never missing a beat and then stuck it back in her bosom. Different. After them came the snake charmer. A man came out with a cane and a couple of cobras wrapped around it. He let them crawl on the floor and played the mizmar for them. I followed the cobra act.

I ended up dancing in several other places, and I swear I had to turn sideways to get on the plane to come home because my head was so swelled.

It was a wonderful adventure, and I met Sohair Zaki who I absolutely adored. She got me up to dance with her, and at that moment, I could have died fulfilled.

Dancing in Egypt.

19 GODDESSES

Belly dancing has been a life-long journey, a journey filled with healing, adventure and fun. The most important aspect of this journey has been my connection with the divine feminine.

I suppose it started that day I felt my ribcage start to move in a circle. It was like something broke loose inside of me, something powerful and potent, something that I had pushed down and hidden and tried to ignore.

As time went on, the shame I had carried with me from the childhood abuse started to lift off of me. As I opened up to my femininity, I began to feel its power and its potential.

At first, I was afraid of those feelings. In fact, I think to some extent, I was fearful for years, but the fear lessened and over time finally disappeared as I became more and more conscious of my own divine aspects.

To me, belly dancing is about the Goddess, but it's not about Goddess worship. I remember my ex-mother-in-law and I both being interviewed by a reporter who asked about the history of the dance. I started to say that the roots of the dance date back to the time of Mother Goddess worship, and I was interrupted by my mother-in-law who was pretty much freaking out and saying, "I want to make it clear, right now that I'm a Christian. I'm not a Goddess worshipper!"

I was talking about the history of the dance and its ancient roots; I wasn't talking about religion. Over time I thought about the whole Goddess thing, and how the Goddess is the female aspect of divinity and how our dance is such a feminine art. And, I began to acknowledge the power of my own femininity.

I've always been somewhat of a feminist, and all for equal rights and equal pay for equal jobs, but at some point I began to see a problem with feminism.

I saw women insisting on being equal by trying to be like men. They even wore dress suits, albeit with skirts, and carried brief cases. They tried to prove they were just as tough and just as strong.

Wait a minute! Hold the presses! What's wrong with this picture?

Women are equal to men, but that doesn't mean they are the same as men, and trying to be the same pretty much defeated the purpose in my opinion!

Our strengths as women don't lie in our musculature but rather in our intuition. We are different than men, and we need to nurture those differences and become empowered in our femininity instead of trying to be more masculine.

I tried to explain my thoughts to one of my Goddess worshipping, feminist friends, and she started to go ballistic. She insisted that we were all the same and that it was societal conditioning that made us different. So, I broke it down for her.

Let's imagine a planet where a female and male child is put with no contact with anyone else. There is no society, no conditioning. They grow up and mate, and the female gets pregnant. Before pregnancy, she may have been able to run as fast as the man, but when she becomes heavy with child, not so much. Now, imagine that while she's giving birth, a saber tooth attacks and the man fights it off. Now, did society condition her to be weaker and him stronger? Of course not, it's just plain genetics. A healthy man will never be as weak and vulnerable as a pregnant woman giving birth, and he will never be able to give birth. Men and women are different physically, and it has nothing to do with society.

Now, this might sound simplistic, but you would be amazed at how many women would argue that we are equal and therefore the same.

The world is out of balance. Patriarchy is dominant, so to me trying to be like men is craziness. I believe that we need to accept our difference, take pride in our femininity and claim our inherent strength as women, and that's the only way we will be able to create a balance of the masculine and feminine.

Over time, as I danced, I began to connect more and more to my own spirituality. I started to feel the divine aspects of myself begin to activate, and I began to see the beauty of my own personal essence and the beauty of each of my sister dancers inside as well as outside.

We are each Goddesses in our own way. We each have the spark of divinity within. Call it Christ light, or Chi or universal life force. The words don't matter. What matters is that all of us are connected by the divine, and as women that expresses as the divine feminine.

As I danced, my heart began to open more and more, and I was able to give and receive more and more love. I have met many, many women through the dance. Some were brief encounters, and some became life-long friendships. It hasn't all been happiness and joy but no matter what, the dance has always been there for me.

When I see a woman quit dancing because of a falling out with another dancer, I feel for her loss. The dance is constant, and the femininity of the dance is eternal.

There is nothing like the power of this art form. It's not just a skill, not just a dance; it's something much deeper, even primal that opens up inside of us and we become a part of something greater than ourselves, something difficult to put into words.

Belly dancing has helped me in body, mind and spirit. It has helped me become comfortable in my own skin, and given me a way to stay physically fit and learn to appreciate my own body. It helped change my negative thinking and overcome depression. And, it helped me connect to my spiritual nature in a strong and powerful way.

It has shown me that my work is with women. I love men, really love them, but my main work is with women. I want to share my passion for dance and healing with them. I want to invite them on this journey to the divine feminine.

During my journey, I have learned that there are only two emotions, love and fear. Everything else stems from these two emotions, and when we are feeling fear, we can't feel love and vise versa. It became my goal to stay loving as much as humanly possible, and that has been my saving grace. What we give is also what we receive. So, believe me when I say, I receive a lot of love!

Once, I label something as a fear, I'm able to overcome it. Fear is all about limitation, and love is all about expansion. I also think of it as a choice. I can choose to live with fear, or I can choose to live with love.

I've also learned that when I do what's best for me, it's also what is best for everyone around me. Doing what is best for me is a form of self-love, and when I love myself I am better able to love others.

I work on staying conscious of these things, choosing love and remembering to choose what is best for me.

The Divine Feminine is always there, inside and out, always present, always powerful. It is up to each of us to individually commit to staying conscious of this aspect of ourselves.

Whenever you have to make a choice, stop and ask, "Am I making this choice based on fear or based on love? And, is this to my own highest good?" Don't make a decision out of fear, and if it's not to your highest good, don't do it. And, I mean, don't do it. Easy to say, I know! I'm still working on it myself.

When you do what is best for yourself, you are staying conscious. As you do this, you will begin to feel better and better, and as you feel better, people in your life will see a difference, and they will begin to feel better just being around you. You will be setting the best example. Know that when you do what is best for you, it will always be what is best for others and ultimately for the world.

Our feminine hips and pelvis are where life begins. We carry the eggs within us. Once the seed is planted, a seed that is too small for our eyes to see without a microscope, we grow life. Yes, we need that teensy, tiny seed, but the rest of the new life is created by us, by our female bodies. It grows inside of us from a microscopic speck into a human being. There is nothing I can think of that is more filled with wonder and Spirit.

When you do hip circles, think of your female body, think about how it makes you feel or made you feel to have the ability to grow a new life inside of you. Whether or not you had children, whether or not you were fertile or unfertile, your body is an expression of the sacred feminine. You *are* the sacred feminine. As we circle our hips and our pelvis, let us imagine that through us, new life begins. We, as women embracing the Divine Feminine have the power to create new life. We have the power to energetically birth a new world for ourselves and collectively for all of humanity.

When you do figure 8's with your hips, the infinity sign, think of the infinite wonder of the divine feminine, and imagine that the divine feminine is within and without and that you have the ability to unleash the power of love into your world bringing healing to yourself and all whom you encounter. You can choose to use this sacred power to help humanity, mother earth and the universe.

As you do rib circles, think of your breasts as a source of nourishment for new life. Our female bodies have the ability to create physical food for our children, and as we nurse and channel milk into their mouths, we also channel our love into their souls. We nourish them physically, emotionally and spiritually.

As women, we nourish the world. We use food, and we use our hearts. As women, we sometimes forget that we also need the nourishment of love and we also need nurturing. So, as you make rib circles, please imagine loving and nurturing yourself. Set up a facial, a massage, do something you love, something joyous. Now, I'd like you to take a moment and imagine how you can channel more love and nurturing into the world. What is it that you can do for yourself, for others, or for the planet that will bring the nourishment of love and nurturing?

We use our dance as a personal expression of our own unique selves, and it's also important to start speaking our truth verbally, to stand up for ourselves and to claim what is to our highest good.

I can only hope that belly dancing gives other women even a fraction of what it's given me, and that those of you who do belly dance take it to the next level, of expressing your true self, a woman of power without shame and without excuses. This is who I am! I am a woman! I am proud! I am beautiful! I am powerful.

And, I hope belly dancing facilitates our connection with other women and all that is feminine to help bring back the balance to our world, and increase the love. For after all, love is the most powerful force in the universe, and it is an eternal force that has been with us for a millennium and will be with us into the future, just as our dance has and will continue.

Dance with the power of the divine feminine; dance with love.

20 FAQ

Isn't belly dance some sort of sex dance performed by harem girls for their man?

Morocco, a world-renowned authority of belly dance puts it this way: "Honey, I can think of a lot easier ways to attract a man; this is something I do for myself!"

I have used it many times over the years, since then, and since men usually ask me this question, I just love popping their bubble of illusion. I'm sorry, I just can't help myself.

Don't belly dancers dance with their bellies?

In reality, stomach rolls and belly undulations involve only a tiny fraction of the dance and many dancers don't even do belly movements. We utilize all of our body parts including our neck, hands and arms, torso, hips and we do lots of different steps.

Don't belly dancers roll coins on their bellies?

In fact, some belly dancers do roll coins on their bellies. It's a specialized talent, more like a circus trick than dancing and my guess is that one in about 10,000 belly dancers might be able to do this.

Do belly dancers really wear jewels in their navels?

Some belly dancers do because they don't know any better or it's a fashion statement. Wearing a jewel in the navel is not a Middle Eastern tradition. It started in Hollywood during the 30's as a form of censorship when navels were considered too risqué to show at the cinema.

Is belly dancing a form of stripping?

When a stripper wears a belly dance costume, she is no more a belly dancer than she is a law officer when she wears a police uniform in her routine.

Isn't belly dancing sexual or lewd?

Real belly dancing is family entertainment. It is a dance that children can do as well as older women. Simply put; if it isn't family appropriate, it isn't belly dancing.

Isn't belly dancing really easy to do?

Just like any other dance form, belly dancing takes a lot of practice and discipline to learn. It is an art form and becoming an expert requires learning steps from around the Middle East as well as the rhythms. A professional must also be able to accompany her dance and the music with zills (finger cymbals).

The next time another type of dancer looks down her nose and declares that belly dancing is so easy, I would like to hand her a pair of zills and tell her to accompany herself while she dances and then tell me how easy that is!

Does belly dancing cause problems in relationships or did belly dancing have anything to do with your divorces?

I don't believe belly dancing causes any problem in a relationship. What sometimes causes a problem is that, as a dancer gains self-confidence, her partner begins to feel threatened. This could happen if she became a champion bowler or knitter. It has nothing really to do with belly dance.

And, yes, belly dancing did have something to do with my first divorce but it was because my husband fell in love with one of my students. That could have happened if I were teaching beading classes, so again, it really had nothing to do with the dance itself.

Does belly dancing have any credibility?

Belly dancing is becoming more and more credible as time progresses. It is important for teachers to have the credentials and experience for quality instruction and education about the dance, rhythms, costuming and history.

Aren't belly dance costumes, really skimpy?

You will see much more skin at the river on a hot day than you'll see at a belly dance event. Most costumes consist of a bra and belt worn with harem pants and a skirt, often vests worn with harem pants and skirts or choli top blouses and harem pants. Some costumes have over 25 yards of fabric.

Don't you have to have a big belly to belly dance?

You don't have to have a certain body type to belly dance. It's not limited like other dance forms; anyone can do it if they have the desire to learn.

Are you afraid to belly dance considering the Middle Eastern terrorism and wars?

Absolutely not. I love being an emissary of the Middle East and helping educate. It's my way of helping bring peace to the world.

Is it true that belly dancing degrades women?

This is an attitude that I have run across and usually comes from misinformed feminist types. I have been told, "It's women like you that get men excited watching you dance, and then they go out and rape other women." I have been told I couldn't do a benefit for a women's shelter because what I did was degrading women and encouraging their victimization.

The reality is that belly dancing empowers women increasing their self-confidence and enhancing their self-image along with the physical benefits of the dance. I have seen it in myself and with so many others. Most women victims, who learn to belly dance, stop acting like victims, stop walking like victims and stop being victims. This is one of my favorite things about the dance.

Any time, I run across any of these myths and attitudes, I use the occasion to EDUCATE. The more we educate, the less people will believe the myths surrounding our dance. For every person we enlighten, they will enlighten others. And, the best way to educate is to show people what we do by volunteering at nursing homes, festivals, benefits, etc. And, every time you volunteer, you are actually advertising which will give you the potential for future paying jobs.

If you have any questions about belly dance, please feel free to email me at mezdulene@mezdulene.com.

A Poem of a Belly Dancer
By Avena Age 9

She's as pretty as a twinkling star.
She belly dances near and far.
I've seen her belly dance before.
But I would like to see her dance even more.
Her outfit is made of colored beads,
And look like little shiny seeds.
She's the best belly dancer I've ever seen.
Her name is Mezdulene.

Dance of the Heart
By Mezdulene

I am a belly dancer.
No longer ashamed of my woman's body;
With it's soft roundness,
and
Its stretch marks from childbearing.

I carry myself with dignity and grace.

I am an Earth Mother:
With ancient rhythms pulsating through my veins.
My dance expresses joy and laughter,
                    sorrow and pain,
                        forgiveness and limitless love.
It is an expression of my inner self:
A celebration of my womanhood,
and
Of life itself.

ACKNOWLEDGEMENTS

I'd like to thank everyone who has been a part of my healing journey, my teachers, my students, my friends and my family. I feel gratitude to each and every one of you.

Special thanks to my daughter, Avena, who believed in me when I didn't believe in myself.

Special thanks to Halima, my mentor, friend, Goddess who has supported me on so many levels and in so many ways over the past 33 years.

Special thanks to Jasel who has been there for me as a friend, dance partner and assistant. She runs things for me when I'm away or ill, and she always believes in me.

Special thanks to my friend, Karen who has helped me integrate so many lessons from my head into my heart.

Special thanks to Mystical Oasis Dance Co. all whom have helped me keep my sanity over the past few years of craziness, each of whom has a special niche in my heart.

Special thanks to Marie who lent me her home in Hawaii where this book was written.

Special blessings to each of you who read this book. May you be inspired, entertained and perhaps even learn a thing or two.

RESOURCES

www.mezdulene.com

www.jareeda.com

www.bellydancerusa.com

ABOUT THE AUTHOR

Mezdulene is a dancer, teacher, seminar instructor and the editor of '*Jareeda*', the longest running belly dance periodical in the world. She is also the sponsor of an annual belly dance retreat for women and the popular Belly Dancer USA competition. She is an ordained minister, Reiki master, Shaman, author and a powerful Divine Feminine Being. Mezdulene lives in Sutherlin, Oregon and is always ready for adventure!